Discover Your Inspiration

Discover Your Inspiration

Real Stories from Real People to
Inspire and Ignite Your Soul

DISCOVER YOUR "I" BOOKS

Discover Your Inspiration
Copyright © 2015 by *Discover Your "I" Books*

All rights reserved. This book or any portion thereof may not be reproduced or transmitted in any form of by any means, graphic, electronic, or mechanical, including photocopying, recording, taping, or by any information storage retrieval system, without the written permission of the publisher except for the use of brief quotations in a book review.

Getting What You Want Publishing

For Information address:

Getting What You Want Publishing
1230 Crescent Dr.
Glendale, CA 91205

in conjunction with

Hybrid Global Publishing
355 Lexington Avenue 8th floor
New York, NY 10017

Without inspiration the best powers of the mind remain dormant. There is a fuel in us which needs to be ignited with sparks.

Johann Gottfried Von Herder

CONTENTS

Introduction   ix
Sue Brooke

1. The Road Trip of Life   1
   Sue Brooke
2. Inspired to Reinvent Myself   9
   Karen Strauss
3. The Daring Young Woman on the Flying Trapeze   15
   Susan Sheppard
4. Embrace Your Pain   23
   Joe DiChiara
5. Choose Bliss   31
   Moneeka Sawyer
6. The Reality of Inspiration   39
   Carolann Hays Wells
7. The Night Out   45
   Sharin Wahlig
8. Diet Is a Four-Letter Word   53
   Kim McLaughlin
9. Keep Talking—Dead People Can't Talk!   61
   Wanda King
10. Damaged Goods   69
    Suzi Fox
11. Childhood Dreams Inspire Grown-Up Service   75
    Kathy Pendleton

Contents

12.	Heal Yourself—Free Your Soul *Sasha Sabbeth*	83
13.	How Good Can Emerge from the Bad *Sheryl Hensel*	91
14.	The Power of Giving *Jason Robins*	99
15.	Blessing in Disguise *Jennifer Darling*	105
16.	Turning the Page at Fifty *Elsie Crowninshield*	113
17.	Cues from the Universe—Believe *Charr Crail*	123
18.	In His Hands *Michelle Calloway*	131
19.	Soaring to New Heights *Nancy Darst*	139

Meet the Authors	147
Become a Featured Author in the Discover Your "I" Book Series	149

INTRODUCTION

You have brains in your head. You have feet in your shoes. You can steer yourself, any direction you choose.

Dr. Seuss

By Sue Brooke, founder of *Discover Your "I" Books*

So . . . what is Inspiration? What does it mean and how can it help us as we travel through our life's journey?

INSPIRATION (in·spi·ra·tion ˌinspəˈrāSH(ə)n/)

- something that makes someone want to do something or that gives someone an idea about what to do or create: a force or influence that inspires someone
- a person, place, experience, etc., that makes someone want to do or create something
- the act of drawing in; specifically: the drawing of air into the lungs

Introduction

- the action or power of moving the intellect or emotions

People like Tony Robbins, Les Brown, Bob Proctor, and Jack Canfield are extremely successful entrepreneurs who make a great living inspiring people. What makes them different?

> The path to success is to take massive, determined actions.
>
> **(Tony Robbins)**

> Everything is out there waiting for you to ask. Everything you want also wants you. But you have to take action to get it.
>
> **(Jack Canfield)**

> You don't have to be great to get started, but you have to get started to be great.
>
> **(Les Brown)**

> When your dreams are strong enough, you will appear to possess super human powers to achieve.
>
> **(Napoleon Hill)**

Do you see a pattern here? Inspiration is only the beginning of your journey from where you are now, to where you want to be. The rest is up to you. The

Introduction

difference you make will be directly related to the actions you take.

Inspiration is most powerful when we hear stories from 'ordinary' people who have done extraordinary things, overcame a great adversity, or did something to help others without expectation. This book is filled with stories from real people who have amazing stories that will be sure to inspire and ignite your soul.

The Road Trip of Life

Sue Brooke

> *"The road we are traveling on could get washed out by a flood or blocked by a landslide, but turning onto the new road could take us to places more beautiful and exciting than we could ever imagine!"*
>
> **Sue Brooke**

As we cruise along on this journey of life, think about it as the most awesome road trip!

Our expedition starts from the time we're born and continues through childhood. We start out as passengers, counting on someone else to steer the ship that will take us on the voyage of our lifetime. Because our parents serve as the drivers in the beginning of our life, it's up to us to stay awake, take in the scenery, and get out and do some exploring along the way. Most importantly, we must pay attention and learn how to steer, when to brake, when step on the gas, and when to slow down!

The Road Trip of Life

The older we get, the more we see, learn, and experience, and the more we begin to slowly take control of the steering wheel. If we have really cool, savvy parents, they'll allow us to take the wheel while we sit on their lap. They'll keep one hand close enough to the controls so they can jump in and take over if we encounter some obstacles or traffic jams along the way.

Some of us aren't as fortunate as others to have parents who are great navigators. Some of us are forced to take the wheel on our own and drive ourselves before we're ready and able to really be in control. Those early drivers must learn on their own, with very little guidance. They can decide to find other drivers who will take control, figure it out and learn on their own, or just park the car and wait for someone to give them a ride.

My father was an amazing driving teacher. He made me learn to drive by parallel-parking a big pickup truck with a four-horse trailer attached! He made sure that both my hands were firmly placed on the steering wheel and I used my rearview mirrors. He made sure I knew where I was going, yet he allowed me to change course if I thought there might be a better way to get there. He also taught me it was okay if I made a wrong turn or hit a curb!

Most importantly, my father taught me to pay attention to the other drivers around me and keep my eye on the road ahead. I wasn't allowed to complain if the road got a little bumpy, it started to rain, or there was a traffic jam because those things helped me become a better driver.

As we cruise along on the road trip of life, it is inevitable that we will run into some bumps, forks in the road, washed-out bridges, and dead ends, but it all makes for an exciting adventure!

Sometimes we allow someone else to dictate which road or which direction we take. It's okay to get someone else's opinion, and it could be a good idea to test out a new route here and there, but just make sure it's the route YOU really want to take.

Some of us get stuck on cruise control. We go along in the same direction because it's easy, comfortable, or we don't want to deviate from the familiar route. Many of us set our GPS to a destination but then forget to pay attention to our surroundings, causing us to miss a hidden path or a new road that hasn't yet been discovered. You don't want to miss out on an opportunity to take a side trip, or stop to see something amazing! Take that windy road that your GPS doesn't recognize. Why not?

As you're going along on your life's journey, the road map you're following will be divided up into chapters. I'm sure we can all identify when one chapter of our life ended and a new one began: childhood, high school, college, job, marriage, kids, or a devastating event such as an illness, divorce, or accident. Usually there is one

The Road Trip of Life

major, life-changing event that forces us to take a completely different route we never planned for, sometimes bringing us to a screeching stop. The key is to get back on the road and keep on moving forward.

The road might get washed out by a flood or blocked by a landslide, but turning onto a new road could take us to places more beautiful and exciting than we could ever imagine!

As you're cruising along on your "road trip of life," when you least expect it, you might hit a dead end. Don't worry! It doesn't mean your trip is over! Most people see dead ends as a negative—they stupidly took the wrong road because they either didn't look at the map or they weren't paying attention. Maybe they got bad directions from someone, or maybe an unexpected tragedy blocked the road temporarily.

Hitting that dead end gives you options for your trip. You can give up and just stop there, or you can turn around and find a new road. If you really want to have fun, you might want to get out of your car and explore a little bit! You never know what you might discover!

I faced my first dead end when my marriage ended. I had given up my career as a teacher, making my dreams and my identity all about my husband and his music career. A few months after we divorced, I was in a very bad car accident. Lying in the hospital bed, I thought I had no friends, because all of my friends were *his* friends. I had no focus in my life anymore, and I didn't know what kind of future, if any, I would have after my recovery. Just when I thought I had nothing left to look forward to, I woke up to a room full of people—people who really cared about me! That day changed my life completely. It took a while to get past the mental and physical pain, but I finally woke up from feeling sorry for myself and made the decision that my life was going to be about *me*—I was going to follow *my* dreams!

We *all* have a story. I thought about writing a book after my "dead end," but I thought, *Why would anyone want to read about* my *life? That would be ridiculous!* I remembered meeting a girl in a wheelchair who had written a book. She was an athlete who had been in a horrible accident that left her paralyzed. Her story was way more compelling than mine could ever be, so why would anyone care about *my* story?

The turning point for me was when I was asked to speak to a group of businesswomen. I had no idea what I was going to speak about, so I decided to begin by sharing how I gained the confidence to change the direction of my life after my failed marriage and car accident.

When I finished speaking, a very strange thing happened: I received emails and phone calls from people who told me I had inspired them and they wanted to hear more!

I thought about the girl in the wheelchair. Yes, her story was very compelling and inspiring because she could overcome such adversity. But to most of us, her story is like a movie—it's interesting and heartwarming, but how many people can really, truly connect with her and know exactly how she feels? On the other hand, I found out that there are a lot more people who connected with my story having had similar stories that were equally captivating.

Our individual stories are real, and I'm pretty sure a pretty large percentage of the human race has gone through and felt many of the same things we have: going through a divorce, having someone close to us die, being in an accident, and so on. It can give us comfort to know that we're not the only ones who have experienced those things.

We are all experts in something or have life experiences that mean something to someone. When we put it all together—where we grew up, who our family is, everyone who has touched our life—every experience makes us so perfectly unique . . . there is no one in the universe exactly like each one of us!

Are there things we experience that may be, let's say . . . challenging? Of course. The key to overcoming those challenges is realizing that every bad or negative thing that happens always ends up turning out to be the very best thing that could have happened! Sometimes it shows up right away, and sometimes it takes a few years.

Sue Brooke

My hope is that along my own life's road trip, I can inspire people like you to look at your own life's road map in a different way, not listen to naysayers, take the controls and map out your own journey, or write your own chapter the way *you* want it written!

About the Author

Sue Brooke is the founder and creator of the *Discover Your "I" Book Series,* an Amazon best-selling author, small business mentor, speaker, coach, and idea innovator.

After surviving a car accident and finding herself with a depleted bank account at the age of forty-four, Sue describes "being hit by a truck" as the moment that changed her life forever. She reclaimed her identity and built several successful businesses, all on her own.

Sue enjoys working with small business owners and entrepreneurs who have dreams of starting a business. She loves marketing and has the unique gift of coming up with innovative ideas and finding opportunities where no one else would think to look.

As a passionate advocate for those who may have lost their identity, she strives to empower and inspire them to live their passion and never give up on their dreams, no matter how crazy they may seem!

Sue believes that everyone has a story that should be told. Giving people an avenue for sharing their own stories, and encouraging others to share theirs, is dream that has come to fruition in her *Discover Your "I" Book* series and Real Stories Books.

Visit her online at http://www.SueBrooke.com. http://www.DiscoverYourI.com

Inspired to Reinvent Myself

Karen Strauss

*Believe with all of your heart that you
will do what you were made to do.*
Orison Swett Marden

To quit or not to quit! That is the question.

I had worked hard in the publishing industry. As a publicist and then later a sales manager, I had worked with many celebrities and *New York Times* best-selling authors. In the early 90s, I had a great job working as a sales director at a major publishing company. I was on the verge of buying a co-op apartment in New York City. I was thirty-four years old and had a great social life.

All good reasons for staying put! On the other hand, I was yearning to go out on my own, break free of corporate walls, and finally start my own business.

Oh yes, I should also mention—I only had about three thousand dollars in the bank. I didn't say I earned a lot of money in this glamorous industry.

I knew that over 50 percent of all small businesses fail within the first five years. *Forbes* said recently that 80 percent of entrepreneurs failed in eighteen months. But for me, failure was not an option. I was young, hungry, and passionate—and I had a very expensive apartment to pay for.

I remember going to my beach house on Fire Island that summer (my favorite place on earth) and, over many glasses of champagne, discussing the pros and cons with my friends. They were incredibly supportive and kept cheering me on to do it. (Maybe it was all that champagne!)

So I took the plunge—I quit my job and set up shop in my very expensive new apartment. So much for new furniture!

My first client was a Christian publisher called Fleming Revell. They were looking to expand their audience from Christians shopping in Christian bookstores to a more general market. My job was to sell their books into large retail stores like Barnes & Noble, Borders, Walden, Costco, and Sam's Club.

As it happened, they owned a small publishing house, Wynwood Press. The editor-in-chief had discovered an unknown author named John Grisham and immediately bought *Time to Kill*. They published the book in hardcover and sold about 5,000 copies. By the time I was on board, John Grisham had published *The Firm* and had become a *New York Times* best-selling author. I was able to take *Time to Kill* into the top retailers and wholesalers and sell about 50,000 copies in a record amount of time. And Fleming Revell had their first *New York Times* best-selling book.

I thought, *Wow! Owning a new business is easy!* I got to sell my first book—a novel written by John Grisham!—to my best friend, the fiction buyer at Barnes & Noble, and the other buyers I had gotten to know well from my other corporate jobs running sales departments at major publishing houses.

I was a hero . . . a genius. A rock star! The Christian publishing company was very impressed with the "nice Jewish girl" they hired from New York City.

This is what I had signed up for. After paying my dues for so long working for someone else—I now had the opportunity to take things into my own hands.

Not so fast! Although this was an amazing start to my new career, it certainly didn't follow a smooth trajectory. Over the years, I have had many ups and downs. I have lost clients that represented over half my revenue. There were many times I just wanted to give up and look for a "steady" job. But I persevered. I changed my mind-set. I decided that I would not give up. Instead of feeling sorry for myself, I was intentional about finding new clients. I knew I was a really good "networker." I always enjoyed meeting people and figuring out how we could work together.

What amazed me was how many of my Christian clients would recommend me to other publishers. That's when it really dawned on me that "reputation" was everything. My name was all I had—and finally my famous bluntness and honesty was being rewarded!

I learned that "cash is king"—there would be months when I made a lot of money and other months when I could barely pay my bills. I needed to roll with the punches and make sure I had enough of a reserve to cover those lean times.

The scariest time came in 2011 when Borders closed. Borders was my biggest account, and I worked on commission. In addition, e-books were on the rise, and I was not paid for e-books sold by Barnes & Noble or Borders. This turn of events was definitely eating into my profits.

I was at a crossroads. The industry was continually changing. The landscape was quite different—Borders had closed, Barnes & Noble was shrinking, and Amazon was gaining market share. It was then I learned that an entrepreneur always needed to be flexible and willing to change. I could not stand still with my business when everything else around me was moving.

I decided to change up my business and concentrate on working with self-published authors to help market their books and get wider distribution.

It was around this time that I met Craig Duswalt. He was speaking in New York City about how to market like a "RockStar," and he inspired me to get out of my comfort zone and travel to Los Angeles to attend his RockStar Bootcamp.

Although I did not know any of the 500 people in the room—I was comfortable with his topic. Marketing yourself and your business to stand out in a crowd begins with publishing a book! Aha! Now we're talking!

I joined his MasterMind program, and it was there that the next idea for a business popped into my head: Create branded publishing companies for organizations. And so Duswalt Press was born. Three years later I created Hybrid Global Press for other individuals and brands that want an alternative to self-publishing.

Starting my own company was the scariest thing I have ever done. I risked everything, but it was also the greatest thing I have ever done. I still get chills when an author campaign is successful. I enjoy working with publishers and authors. I feel rewarded when my clients are happy.

I now understand that, while it's not an easy road, for me it was the most exhilarating and satisfying path I could have taken.

About the Author

Karen Strauss has held management and marketing positions at major publishing houses such as Crown, Random House, and Avon. Strauss Consultants works with authors and other organizations to maximize sales and marketing potential. She is the author of *Book Publishing for Entrepreneurs: Top Secrets from a New York Publisher.*

www.StraussConsultants.com

www.hybridglobalpublishing.com

THE DARING YOUNG WOMAN ON THE FLYING TRAPEZE

Susan Sheppard

"Those who don't jump will never fly."
Leena Ahmad Almashat

Many years ago I started on a journey of self-discovery. I had just delivered my third daughter, and was struggling with the excess weight I gained with each pregnancy. I had a great job as the department manager of a pediatric unit specializing in endocrine and neurosurgical-compromised children. I had been asked to open this new department and train the nurses to take care of babies and small children. I loved being a manager and making a real difference in the care being delivered.

And then I began to notice a strange physical symptom: I felt like I was choking all the time. I went to see my doctor, a friend of mine named Jim. He said the sensation was probably due to the stress of my job since he was familiar with the insanity I dealt with on a daily basis. He added, "However, it would be embarrassing to miss a diagnosis, so let's do some tests."

The test results showed I had severe hypothyroidism. He put me on Synthroid and then said, "What are we going to do about your weight? I took a course recently, and a lot of the participants lost weight after completing it."

I said, "Okay, I'll do it!" And so I signed up for Lifespring, my very first personal growth seminar. I absolutely loved it. It was a confrontational, fun, experiential, loving, experience—and it scared the shit out of me.

I went to the seminar alone, not knowing a soul, and I made friends there that I still have today, almost forty years later. The result of that basic, advanced, and three-month TC (training coordinator) program was a 100-pound weight loss in ninety days. I was amazed that a short-lived program could make that kind of difference. But it did.

I immersed myself in the culture with the other graduates of this training, and for three years I maintained my weight loss and totally enjoyed the safety and support of that nurturing, close circle of friends. I almost went to work for Lifespring, but taking that job would have resulted in 50 percent pay cut from my managerial position in the hospital. At that point I decided that

I needed to use what I had learned in a larger way, so I withdrew somewhat from the community and took my knowledge and insights out into the world.

It was a reality check that I did not expect. I felt like I was in enemy territory. People in the real world were not ready for enlightenment and accountability.

I was shocked.

I was determined to continue my personal growth quest. My next experience was with Anthony Robbins. I wanted to walk on hot coals and learn how to have the life I wanted. I went to his weekend event, and I did walk on hot coals. It was a great, fulfilling, inspiring experience. Again I immersed myself in the culture with the group of friends I bonded with at his training. We decided to enroll in Tony's NLP-certification program, which was taking place in Texas over a two-week period.

Arriving in Austin, Texas, we embarked on a marathon of learning and craziness. We started every morning with yoga at 7:00 a.m. and ended usually anywhere between midnight and 2:00 a.m.

Tony was on stage about 95 percent of the time. He had seemingly limitless energy. We learned about NLP (neuro linguistic programming), Ericksonian hypnosis, the vegetarian lifestyle, and how to have endless energy because energy is choice. It was a fabulous learning experience, and I wouldn't trade it for the world.

The one really challenging event for me was climbing a 60-foot high telephone pole, jumping from the pole to a trapeze, and slowly being lowered to the ground.

There were seven hundred participants in this certification program, and I was not one of the youngsters. At forty-seven years of age and once again a good 80 pounds overweight, I was terrified. There was absolutely no way that I would pass on the experience, but I just didn't know how I was going to accomplish such a herculean task.

For several days during my lunch break, I watched as participant after participant attempted to climb the pole and at one point or another fell off the pole. Of course, we had safety lines and were completely protected, but how did people actually do this feat? Tony had repeatedly reminded us of his guaranteed success plan which was to have a clear outcome, develop a strategy to follow, and do what is in front of you until you achieve your goal. I knew I could do this—but how?

I continued to watch and see what strategy I should adopt and follow. The petite 100-pound athletic types had very little difficulty. They looked like cats climbing the pole and easily stepping onto the top. Taller people would get to the top and attempt to hold onto the top of the pole, which would throw them completely off balance and cause them to topple to the ground. One helicopter pilot who could fly with no doors on his chopper couldn't get more than a third of the way up the pole without freezing.

It was beginning to look like my short, rotund body was really going to be challenged. We had been divided into teams, and most of my team members were fit athletes, much younger than me and in better shape.

On the fifth day of observing, I had a flash of genius. I knew I could climb the pitons one at a time, staying focused and present to only what was in front of me. My challenge was getting on top of the pole. My insight was that I could let go, stand up, and walk the last three or four pitons as though I were walking up stairs. I could use the guideline rope that hung from a ring above the top to maintain my equilibrium. With that I had a clear strategy. I was excited now, and I knew I could do it.

Our team's turn came on the eighth day. My teammates were very supportive but doubtful about my success. I was grinning inside, though, because I knew I had an outcome, a strategy, and a plan to stay present.

It was finally my turn to get strapped into the harness and do my climb. It was an absolutely incredible experience. I walked to the pole. I repeated a little success mantra and started climbing, reminding myself to only pay attention to what was in front of me. Step after step, I climbed until I was three feet from the top of the pole. I stopped and looked around, and then I reached up with my right hand and lightly grasped the rope that was attached to my harness and strung through the ring above me. I let go of the pole with my left hand and stood up straight. I took one step and then a second step with my left foot. I stepped onto the top of the pole with my right foot, then stood up straight on both feet and stretched out my arms. My team was screaming riotously with joy, and I was crying. For at least 60 seconds, I reveled in the joy of my accomplishment, and as the trapeze swung toward me, I jumped. I caught the trapeze and was lowered to the ground with my harness and guide rope.

This may not sound like much of an accomplishment—or maybe even a little silly for grown adults to be doing—but for me, a forty-seven-year-old mother of three who was out of shape and overweight, with very little athleticism left, it was like winning a gold medal in the Olympics. To this day, it is a stellar reminder of how I do anything is how I do everything. In addition, Tony's "outcome, strategy, action" philosophy has served me daily since that fateful day in 1990.

Today, I am retired from nursing, I'm maintaining my latest 100-pound weight loss, and I still save lives—but in a very different way. I work with women who have wounded or broken hearts to heal them and help them to find their true love relationship. Using my original Love with CLASS system, I provide my clients with a clear outcome and a step-by-step strategy to heal, grow, expand their comfort zone, and choose the man they want to spend the rest of their life loving. Any woman can visit and schedule a magical inquiry with me at *www.GettingWhatYouWant.com* to see if what I do can help overcome her fear.

About the Author

Susan Sheppard is the founder of Getting What You Want, Inc., a life and relationship coaching organization created to teach sacred intimacy in all personal relationships. She is the author of the books *How to Get What You Want From Your Man Anytime* and *Dating After 40: No More Excuses*.

Susan's forty years as a registered nurse in emergency services has honed her crisis intervention skills as a coach, author, and speaker whose mission is to replace fear with love by her courageous conversations, inspired writing, and honesty. She is on a mission to get people loved the way they want to be loved. She has a track record of helping people meet their perfect partner and find true intimacy, love, and commitment.

Truly a renaissance woman, she has been a partner or founder of nine different businesses in many different industries. You can visit Susan at www.GettingWhatYouWant.com.

EMBRACE YOUR PAIN

Joe DiChiara

*"Start by doing what's necessary;
then do what's possible; and suddenly
you are doing the impossible."*

St. Francis of Assisi

Inspiration: The process of being mentally stimulated to do or feel something, especially to do something creative.

Inspiration can come from many places. Being awed by God's beauty, a baby's laugh, a pretty woman's smile. These are all stimulating events and by definition can be inspiring. For me, my greatest inspirations have come during some of my darkest hours. Who would have thought that these periods would prove to be the most beneficial of my life?

Someone once said that pain is the touchstone of spirituality. But why do we need to go through pain to grow? No pain, no gain, right? I thought that only applied to physical workouts, but it turns out to be a universal law that applies to everything. In *A Road Less Traveled*, M. Scott Peck writes in the first line of the first chapter: "Life is difficult." He goes on to explain that once you accept that life is difficult, life stops being difficult. When you accept this universal fact, you can view pain as an opportunity to grow and embrace it for what it really is.

Pain Is Inevitable—Suffering Is Optional

Complaining about life's situations and conditions brings suffering. Such self-inflicted wounds grow, only to bring more suffering and more complaining. Individuals that refuse to accept the fact that life is tough allow all kinds of mental and physical ailments into their systems, causing even more suffering. These people drift aimlessly through life, settling for whatever life throws at them.

    I didn't want to be one of them, and thus I learned one of the most important words in the dictionary of success: *tenacity*. People fail time and time again, but that doesn't make them failures. The only failures are the people who give up. You can decide not to be a failure. You can choose to be tenacious.

    On the way to becoming tenacious, I went through plenty of pain: my brother's suicide, my sister's murder, leaving my family, bankruptcy, alcohol and drug addiction . . . These were all very difficult experiences, and I suffered dearly because I didn't know the truth. And the truth is simple: Life is tough; get over it.

I chose to be tenacious and embrace this simple truth, so when I entered one of those dark periods of my life in 2015, I knew it was going to be one of those growing experiences. Financially, mentally, and spiritually, this was one of the most painful times in my life.

At the beginning of that year, I walked away from over half of a successful accounting practice. I knew there would be plenty of challenges, but I was ready—or so I thought. The decision did not come suddenly; it had been building for over a year. And while there was only so much I could do to minimize the severe financial challenges I knew I would face, I made a decision a long time ago that I would be very selective with the people I do business with. Through a series of unavoidable circumstances, I found myself having to advise some unsavory characters as well as other individuals I respected but who ran sloppy businesses. Sloppy inevitably turns into problems, and problems like that wind up costing me time and money. Unfortunately these individuals were some of my largest clients. I had no choice but to leave if I wanted to stick to my principles, and I believed that if I did, the Universe would send me more of the right kind of clients. However, the Universe doesn't always respond immediately, and that's where tenacity comes into play.

Embrace Your Pain

Knowing life is tough and accepting that fact doesn't make pain any less painful. It hurts, and this time it hurt a lot. There were the obvious, expected financial adversities. I cut back on all nonessential expenses, refocused on the services that brought in quick cash, and let go of all of my pie-in-the-sky, greatest ideas ever. I had been there before plenty of times and always persevered. What caught me by surprise this time was the mental turmoil and spiritual lapses I experienced.

My family had gotten comfortable with dining out often, receiving nice gifts during holidays and birthdays, and other luxuries. It's not that they gave me any grief about the new austerity program; it was all self-inflicted guilt. I caused my own suffering despite everything I had learned about pain and suffering.

Then there were my friends and the people I had been doing business with for years. Suddenly I was absent, and for no apparent reason. This caused more self-inflicted guilt and suffering. Then came the surprising spiritual lapses. I stopped praying. I stop communicating with the Spirit of the Universe I had been so close to for so long. I started questioning myself: *Could I have done things differently? Had I made a major blunder?*

The rise or fall of everything usually starts little by little. A change in a good habit, feeling sorry for yourself, not eating right, lack of exercise are all little cracks in the foundation of a prosperous life. Before you know it, your whole life is falling apart—as if it happened suddenly, all at once. This time was supposed to be different. This time I had self-awareness and knowledge. I thought I was prepared. I wasn't—or maybe I was.

The turning point came on a cold day in March while I was walking my dog Winston. As I was cursing the cold wind and being annoyed at him for making me go out in this weather, a thought occurred to me. Was I tenacious or not? You can't be tenacious some of the time. You're either tenacious all of the time, or you're a quitter. I was not a quitter. I had proved that over the years. I always came out of adversity strong.

Pain can also be a terrific motivator. As I watched Winston hop around the snow and ice, a feeling of great inspiration came over me. All at once my faith came back, my mind-set turned from negative to positive, and even my posture and the way I was walking changed. I was energized because I *knew* I was tenacious. Positive thoughts and ideas flooded my mind again. Instead of reacting to each challenging occurrence, I became proactive in my solutions.

Where were the untapped revenue streams? What bills could I pay now? What did my budget look like? How much did I need to bring in to get into the black again? A bad attitude and negative mind-set had blurred my vision. A mental fog hides easy solutions, and now the fog was lifted. I felt a new freedom and suddenly saw great opportunities all around me—opportunities that

Embrace Your Pain

had been there all along but invisible when I was mired in my self-inflicted suffering. Suddenly I recognized the pain for what it was: an opportunity for serious growth. Now I embraced the pain and thought, *Bring it on! I'm ready for you, pain, and you don't scare me!*

Where did this inspiration come from? It came from the same place everything comes from—The Spirit of the Universe. It's always there if we know how to connect to it. Self-pity and suffering makes that connection hard, if not impossible. Sometimes it takes a jolt, a slight change of direction, or in my case, a word: *tenacity.*

By June 2015 I was back in the black. I came out a new man, a man who had grown mentally, spiritually, and financially. I had a new freedom and a new happiness. With my new positive attitude, new doors opened.

Inspiration creates action and opportunities. If pain is inevitable, then why not embrace it? Why not be inspired by it?

About the Author

Joe DiChiara is an accomplished CPA and entrepreneur with over thirty years of experience working with thousands of small businesses. He specializes in start-ups, growing businesses, and enterprises in distress. After graduating with a BS in accounting in 1984, Joe quickly developed strong managerial and problem solving skills. He opened his first CPA office in 1994, specializing in solving individual and business tax problems.

In 2004 Joe developed an online bookkeeping system that reduced the time needed to operate his accounting practice by over 50 percent while reducing client accounting costs by up to 25 percent. In 2007 he began teaching his system to individuals with no prior bookkeeping skills, resulting in several of his students successfully launching their own bookkeeping businesses.

Joe developed his own philosophy for personal and entrepreneurial success called The Bedrock Business Builders Success System. He trained for over four years to become a speaker, author, and business coach in order to teach his system to entrepreneurs throughout the world. You can visit Joe at www.bedrockbusinessbuilders.com.

CHOOSE BLISS

Moneeka Sawyer

> *"I am responsible. Although I may not be able to prevent the worst from happening, I am responsible for my attitude toward the inevitable misfortunes that darken life. Bad things do happen; how I respond to them defines my character and the quality of my life. I can choose to sit in perpetual sadness, immobilized by the gravity of my loss, or I can choose to rise from the pain and treasure the most precious gift I have—life itself."*
>
> **Walter Anderson**

It was moving day. I was twenty-two years old, and beginning my next adventure.

My white Geo Prizm was packed with all my belongings—as many boxes and clothes as I could fit for this trip to my new apartment. I was on my way to Santa Clara, excited about what was ahead.

It was rush hour, and I was on the main drag, the San Thomas Expressway, five lanes in one direction, barely

Choose Bliss

moving. I didn't mind. I turned up the radio and sang along to "Forever Young," enjoying the adventure.

I was three cars back from the stoplight. Stopped. Waiting. Singing along.

Without warning, my car imploded.

I heard the screech of tires and the sound of metal crumpling. As my dashboard was pushed back into my chest, the rear of my car propelled me forward. My body was crushed as the car compacted like an accordion, glass exploding everywhere around me. If it were not for the boxes packed in tight behind me, I don't know if I would have survived.

Somehow, in a daze, I pushed the driver's side door open and got out of the car. I began picking up my belongings, which were strewn all over the expressway, while cars whizzed past me.

"Honey. Honey! You need to stop." A woman had pulled over and approached me.

"No, no. Just one more thing," I said, barely coherent, blood trickling down my cheek.

She kindly ran out and grabbed whatever treasure I had pointed at, then guided me to the curb.

When the fire trucks arrived, a fireman sat down next to me and started asking me questions. I was in shock and couldn't speak.

"Do you know where you are? Do you know your name?"

I just nodded.

"Sweetie, please don't move your head." Later I learned they were afraid I had broken my neck.

I nodded again. He held my head between his hands and asked me another question.

I couldn't talk. I started to cry.

While the fireman was still trying to get me to respond, the driver of the white Cadillac that rear-ended me approached.

"When are we going to be done with this?" he said. "I didn't need this tonight. I'm already late for a date with my fiancée."

When I arrived at the hospital, I still hadn't found my voice, so no one had been contacted or even knew what had happened to me.

Eventually I woke up to see my brother at my bedside. I was in a haze from all the painkillers. Now that I was awake, the doctor came in to tell me about my condition.

"Your legs have been seriously damaged. They aren't broken, but both your hips are dislocated, and your knees are terribly swollen. We're not sure how you're going to recover, and you'll never be able to walk the same again."

The doctor said that they were ordering a wheelchair for me because I'd be incapacitated for a while.

"What's the process for getting me out of the wheelchair?" I asked, fighting to comprehend what he was telling me.

"We'll figure that out later. For now, we just want to manage your pain."

"Absolutely not," I said. "We're going to figure this out without a wheelchair."

I was bound and determined to walk again. Not only that, but I had danced for seventeen years, and I was going to dance again.

Within two months, I was able to endure being upright, either sitting or standing, for an hour or two at a time. After six months, I was finally able to "walk," which actually meant shuffling around, usually holding onto something. But even after two years of being on significant pain medication and receiving ongoing physical therapy, the constant pain still had not gone away. Sitting was extremely painful, and at night I would cry myself to sleep.

If I didn't take the drugs, I couldn't sleep. If I took the drugs, I couldn't function—my brain would be all muddled.

Until the accident I had dreams of becoming a professional dancer, so I practiced dance two hours a day. I had just graduated from business school and was on my way to start a brand-new corporate job that I was very excited about. As you can see, I had prepared myself for all the things I thought were going to bring me bliss. Then real life happened.

After the accident I gained a huge amount of weight. I could barely walk, much less dance. Any dreams I had of professionally dancing completely disappeared.

My dreams and my life were shattered.

I was barely able to keep my head above water at my job. My fiancé, who I loved madly, left me because the constant pain had turned me into a bitter, cranky, angry, frustrated person who was always yelling at him.

Still I kept pushing forward; I refused to give up. But eventually the pain took its toll on me and depression took over. I felt hopeless, intensely alone, and desperate. Bliss was no longer a concept that had any place in my life at that point. But I knew that there had to be something better.

I tried all sorts of things to improve my life. I was on pain killers constantly to keep the pain at bay. I went on antidepressants and tried all kinds of therapy. I surrounded myself with friends whose lives were filled with drama so I could distract my mind from my own pain.

I accumulated all the stuff that I thought would make me feel fulfilled: big house, cars, clothes, jewelry. I often spent beyond what I could afford, but hey, I deserved it, right? I needed something to make me happy!

None of it worked. It didn't get me to the place I really wanted to be, which was happy inside. And one day I became so despondent, so fed up, so crushed that, in a fit of desperation, I made a decision.

I still can hear that voice in my head. "It's over. This life is over. I can't do this anymore. If I don't change, I will die. I have to do something *now!*"

Choose Bliss

On that sunny morning in May, I decided that I was willing to give up everything—my whole life as I knew it and everything in it—to find the happiness, peace, and contentment I so desperately wanted. And just like that, I decided I was going to go after it.

So what did I do at that point? I stopped looking outside of myself for things that might make me happy. I started to dance and bring movement back in my life. It was intensely painful, and I had to start very slowly, but without dance I felt like I wasn't living. I started to do the necessary internal work in order to find the root cause of my misery. I did meditation, breath work, and lots of soul-searching.

I had been on a spiritual growth path since I was sixteen, but with the accident I had been derailed. Now it was time for me to return to that path. I went back to the basics and brought those things I had learned so long ago back into my life.

Through this journey, what I found is that bliss is not an emotion. It's a way of being. I discovered that no matter what I was going through, I had a choice about whether to be miserable or choose to be at peace and in joy no matter what.

Life had shown me that things can go wrong, very wrong, and that no matter what I plan for or do, things can happen that can change everything. I needed to be able to rely on myself to support my own bliss. And I could only do that by managing my choices, my thoughts, and my own internal strength.

Today my life is so much more amazing than I could have ever imagined. I have been happily married to the man of my dreams for over two decades. I live in a beautiful house; I have wonderful friends and amazing relationships with my family. I have a thriving business, and I get to spend each day doing what I love most, which is helping other people find their own bliss. I travel the world and have been to over fifty countries, just because I wanted to experience all those different kinds of people and cultures. My external life is rich with adventure, playfulness, joy, and comfort. My internal life is content, passionate, and filled with the joy of living.

I feel so blessed to have been able to come this far. Along the way I've learned a thing or two about what works and what doesn't, and I've shared that in my book *Choose Bliss: The Power and Practice of Joy and Contentment.* Because I know what it means to suffer in this world, I've dedicated my life to sharing what I've learned with as many people as I can. No matter what painful experiences someone encounters, I know that bliss is possible—I'm living proof!

About the Author

Moneeka Sawyer has often been described as one of the most joyful people you will ever meet. She finds her bliss through helping people live a life filled with meaning, purpose, passion, and joy. She has been coaching in the Silicon Valley for over ten years, and her unique approach has helped clients from artists and soloprenuers to high-tech CEOs discover their own personal definition of bliss and create a whole new sense of power, energy, and excitement about their businesses and their lives. She shares her life and her joy with her wonderful husband, David, and their adorable Pomeranian in Mountain View, California.

Find Moneeka at www.CoreBlissLife.com.

THE REALITY OF INSPIRATION

Carolann Hays Wells

"I am not afraid of storms, for I am learning how to sail my ship."

Louisa May Alcott

Inspiration is everywhere! All you really need to do is open your eyes and your heart to find inspiration. It is literally all around you.

I love to hear people's stories—where they came from, how they got to where they are now, where they're going. I especially like to hear these stories from strangers. When I travel, I am always inspired. The reality is that every single person and animal that has touched my life has inspired me in some way.

Strippers inspire me! You might wonder why. Well, it's because we don't know their story! They're not "bad" people, and none of us have walked a day in their

The Reality of Inspiration

shoes. They usually make a pretty good living, and they are incredibly fit. (Have you ever tried to actually work a stripper pole?)

My husband bought me one for Christmas one year, at my request. Let me tell you, working that dang pole is *not* easy! I had a fortieth birthday party for him, and everyone tried it—and most failed. The men actually did better than the women! It takes amazing strength, and consider the emotional separation the stripper must maintain to be up on that stage.

I remember trying to master a particular move on the pole; I was frustrated because I just couldn't get it. My husband came in and *nailed* the move. That wasn't super inspiring, but we had a good laugh and that *was* inspiring! Why? Because he humored me; he bought me that pole, and then he helped me! Inspiration!

No, Mom, I've never been a stripper, but I did aspire to be one for a while (wink)! Speaking of my mom, of all of the people on earth, she has inspired me the most. Growing up she had a career (when women mostly stayed home with the kids), she cared for the family, and made amazing meals every single day. She has always been my biggest supporter and encourages me daily. After the loss of my dad, she has grown into an even more inspiring woman. She is kind, caring, smart as a whip, considerate, loving, and the most beautiful woman I know. I've always said, "If I could be half the woman my mom is, I'd be an amazing woman!"

My brother Tom inspired me. My big brother was the guy that could charm anyone and make a million dollars one day and lose it the next! I'm laughing as I type that, but it's really true. His addiction was bigger than he was, unfortunately. No one wants to talk about that kind of stuff, but it's real life. Tom inspired me because I know where *not* to go. It's a really crappy life lesson, but a lesson well learned the hard way.

My friend Sheryl inspires me because she follows her dreams, even if she doesn't know exactly what her dream is at the time! She goes, and she does, and she *is*! I like to call her my favorite gypsy! Find a friend that encourages your outrageousness! Find the friend that says, "Yes, do it; be that!" That's a true friend—the kind that pushes you out of your comfort zone and encourages you to follow that crazy dream you have.

And then follow where your heart is leading you! If your heart says, "Be an accountant," then do it! If your heart says, "Be a minister," then pursue that, and don't let anyone deter you. And if your dream is to be a stripper, then go for it—just don't tell your mom I told you!

Cancer fighters inspire me! They are brave beyond belief. I don't say that lightly; I remember clearly my husband saying, "Game on, babe," when he started chemo nearly ten years ago. I sat by him, sobbing as they started his first infusion, and *he* consoled *me*. He fought the cancer, and he won. Our kids were young at the time, and they were brave little soldiers. Watching someone you love endure treatment is no easy task; it's devastating and scary. In a weird sense I'd say cancer itself has inspired me. I've made changes in my life that I'm certain I wouldn't have made had I not experienced the disease in my family.

My dad also battled cancer—he was a brave and strong fighter the entire time. Even when he was at the very end of his life, he was inspiring! The hospice nurse asked him, "Mr. Hays, what's one thing you'd like to do before you die?" Without missing a beat, he looked at her and said, "That's none of your business!" I'm laughing right now—he was sassy until his last breath! What he wanted to do was go deer hunting on the farm with "his boys"; he didn't make it for that, but I'm certain he was with them in the woods opening morning. My dad still inspires me on a daily basis. When you lose someone you love, you've only lost the human person—his or her spirit is with you always. You just need to open up and let them in.

The reality is, life isn't easy. The old cliche, "No one gets out alive," is real and true. So let's make the *best* of the time we have here instead of watching the news, listening to the news, reading the news . . . Instead, let's just *be*! Being is freeing!

Sometimes *I* inspire myself. When business is tough and money is tight, it's challenging. Those times inspire me to do better, try harder, figure it out, and keep moving forward. When I look back and reflect on how I've dealt with tough times, I'm inspired!

No one else can tell you what your "life purpose" should be. I've been trying to figure that out for years. I still don't know what it is! What I can say, though, is that I've learned to be grateful for my life, even when life sucks. I'm grateful that I can learn from those times! I've learned to forego the pity party, quit sniveling about how crappy my day is, and open my eyes, my mind, and my heart to the gift of life I've been given. I've learned to face those darn challenges that I really would rather not face. The faster I face them, the faster they're fixed!

I find inspiration every day, even if it's something small. One of my favorites is the smell of coffee in the morning. It inspires me to get up and get going!

Embrace the wonder in your life every single day. Take that break, watch those birds, listen to the ocean, pet your dog or cat, hug people, smile at strangers, smell those flowers—and most of all, know you really are enough, so love yourself and be inspired! You'll be glad you did.

About the Author

Carolann's dream world includes successful family businesses and her continued career as a stay-at-home dog mom! When she no longer keeps the books at the business, she will sit by the water writing whatever suits her fancy that day, and delve deeper into her yoga practice.

As a writer she has written for TV, print, radio, web, and social media.

When she isn't cookin' the books at the shop, writing stories about her dog Ziggy, or writing romantic tales, she enjoys spending time with her family and friends, plant-based cooking that make meat eaters' mouths water, being aboard her boat, and traveling.

THE NIGHT OUT

How I received $160 in
One Night Without Asking for a Dime

Sharin Wahlig

"What you focus on, you get more of."
Napoleon Hill

"People are rude."
"People are mean."
"People are selfish."
"People can't be trusted."
"Don't talk to strangers."
"People are greedy."
"People don't care."

If these are the beliefs we hold in our minds, if these are the limiting beliefs that have been passed down to us throughout our lives, and if "like tends begets like," isn't this what we will find more of?

I've long believed that inspiration is everywhere—all we have to do is look. So when I learned I had the opportunity to contribute a story in a book about discovering your "inspiration," I thought it was the perfect time to share the story of a night I will remember and be inspired by for the rest of my life.

Several years ago, I was in an intense thirty-day training program to become a success coach for a Anthony Robbins. One night we were challenged on the spot to go from San Diego to Los Angeles and back in less than twenty-four hours; the trick was that we had to leave behind all our everyday conveniences: food, money, phone, credit cards, shelter, and transportation. Oh, and by the way, we left at 11:00 p.m. Our only instructions were to make a difference in service to others, have fun, and contribute along the way. The women were allowed to travel in pairs, so I buddied up and off we went.

Our first stop was a hotel hotspot where the bar was still flooded with local nightlife. Much to my amazement I ran into a young lady, Rachael, who ironically earlier that week I had met at a mall smoking. I offered to coach her for free and help her break the smoking habit she said she no longer wanted. She agreed, and I offered her the opportunity to receive world-class breakthrough coaching from our iconic coach. She was very grateful for the gift, so she offered to take us to the train station, only to find it closed. Still wanting to help, she said, "I want to give you some money for your journey," and handed me all she had left in her purse, and then dropped us off at the hotel. I was so inspired that this young lady would go out of her way in the middle of the night to help us out. *People are kind and generous!* I thought.

Still needing to get to Los Angeles, I approached the hotel's valet, Adam. *He works around cars—maybe he could take us,* I thought. We had a great conversation, and I also offered to coach him for free after he told me he loved Anthony Robbins' work and had been studying it recently. He was unable to take us to Los Angeles, so I asked him if I could borrow his car.

"Well, I would let you take it, but it's an older Mercedes and I would worry if it broke down on the freeway. You don't have any money or a phone, and I'd hate for you to get stranded, but I want to help you. If you can wait until my shift ends, I'll take you to my house and give you some money."

True to his word, after he was finished with work, he took us to his home. I was shocked when he came back to the car and handed me eighty-five dollars—no questions asked. I expressed my gratitude and invited him to come to the office the following evening and meet Tony Robbins in person. He was thrilled, to say the least. I was incredibly inspired that this total stranger

The Night Out

had been so kind—willing to let us borrow his car (had it been more reliable) and giving us way more money than we ever expected. *Strangers really do help each other out*, I thought.

At the bus station, with nearly enough money for a ride to Los Angeles, we encountered a self-educated young man from Mexico. He and his girlfriend had just broken up, so he was taking a train ride up the coast to clear his head. I offered him some coaching to ease his heartache, and then, in gratitude, he opened his wallet and said, "Here, I'd like to give you some money. Every time I leave home, I fill my wallet with one-dollar bills so I can give to the homeless; today I am considering you my homeless!" He handed me several of his one-dollar bills. I was amazed that such a young man would consciously think of others on a day when he was personally heartbroken. *People are so unselfish and caring!*

When the bus arrived we boarded with a large group of teenagers. Along the way I learned about the adventure they were on. They were from a high school in Northern California and had raised enough money to build a house for a family in Mexico. They worked all year to raise the money, and this particular weekend they went to Mexico, met the family, and participated in building their home. They shared a story of another family they saw with a broken down truck on the side of the road. They wanted to help, but they knew the father would be too proud to take their money, so the kids all got together and pitched in their leftover lunch money, put it in a Bible with a note, and gave it to the stranded family. I was so inspired by how selfless this group of teenagers were. *Teenagers are so polite, generous, helpful, and amazing!*

As we arrived in LA, we were laughing and talking about going to Disneyland. "We're supposed to have fun! What's more fun than the Happiest Place on Earth?" A family overheard us talking and offered to drive us. I couldn't believe it. We hopped in their car with trust and total faith. During our drive to Disneyland, I sat next to their four-year-old son, who I learned had been sick with a life-threatening illness his whole life. The family struggled to take care of him, yet they shared examples with us of how they give back. The father and his brother ride their bikes for charity. I was incredibly inspired by how selfless they were—doing so much for others especially when they themselves are burdened with hardship in their own family. *People really do care!* I thought.

Back in San Diego, our final stop was one of the most inspiring encounters I have ever had. Sitting next to me was a young lady dressed in hospital scrubs. She shared that she was a single mom on her way to see her parents who were homeless drug addicts living on the streets. "I visit them every week and bring them toothpaste, toothbrushes, food, and supplies. I knew I wanted more for myself, so I put myself through school

The Night Out

and became a nurse. Now I am continuing my medical education and working towards becoming a doctor." What an amazing evening filled with unexpected inspiration everywhere I turned!

"People are polite."
"People are kind."
"People are selfless."
"People can be trusted."
"People are generous, and willing to help."
"People are giving."
"People *do* care!"

Sharin Wahlig

About the Author

Author, Speaker, Trainer, Coach

Her desire for independence and her passion to make a difference has lead **Sharin Wahlig** down the road of entrepreneurialism. She began her career in the corporate arena, cultivating expertise in sales, management, and leadership but found true joy in being an entrepreneur while inspiring others to find and live their passion.

Sharin has trained and mentored hundreds of individuals in business and personal life across the country, from stages or on a one-on-one basis. She is the founder and creator of live events and systems—Live Life by Your Design, Because You Can; Because Ladies Can; and Finding Your Happiest Path to Cash—where she teaches and inspires others to Live Their Best Life Now.

During her career as an entrepreneur, she helped launch and grow two start-up companies to multimillion dollar status (which are still in operation today) by creating and implementing systems to develop successful leadership teams, women's organizations, sales teams, and Wow Factor event planning.

Nicknamed the "DreamKeeper," today, with her Juicy Jar System, Sharin assists others to have more fun while getting more done so they can spend quality time doing even more of what they enjoy.

DIET IS A FOUR-LETTER WORD

Kim McLaughlin

> *"In spite of the fact that 90–95% of all diets fail, you tend to blame yourself, not the diet! Isn't it ironic that with a massive failure rate for dieting, we don't blame the process of dieting?"*
>
> **Evelyn Tribole, MS, RD, and Elyse Resch, MS, FADA,** *Intuitive Eating*

Pictures do not lie. You could literally see it on my face—there was a dramatic change in how I looked from one grade to the next. I had definitely gained weight. How could this have happened in such a short period of time? I remember my obsession with food starting then, too—the constant thought about what I would eat; the worry that I might not get enough. Wondering when I could get more; sneaking food when no one was looking. My mom asking, "Do you really want more?" I heard this as criticism: "Do you really *need* more?" The answer I told myself was, "Yes, I need more." I did not verbalize this, because then I would be telling the truth. This was my secret. It was not a well-kept secret, since the overeating showed up on my body, in the size of my clothes, and on my face. Food was my comfort and security. It felt good in a world that was out of my control.

My parents divorced when I was eight years old. My mom, brother, and I moved from our home in Southern California to an apartment in Northern California's Silicon Valley. There wasn't any anger or yelling in my parents' house—just a quiet ending of a marriage and a family unit.

I began to manage my feelings by overeating. Feelings of sorrow, loneliness, worry, fear, and sadness subsided for a while with food. Like so many overweight children, I was teased about my weight. I remember to this day some of what was said to me and about me. It was horrible to be called names, to be judged based on the size of my body.

It was demoralizing and shaming to have to hide food, to sneak it, to be afraid if someone saw me eating. But I figured if I hid what I was eating and ate when no one was looking, maybe I could avoid the truth my heavier body was telling me.

In my early teens I began what would be years of dieting. My mom was concerned about her weight, and she dieted, too, so she invited me to join her on a high-protein diet. I agreed, and thus began my dieting journey. I still recall my first "diet plate" consisting of a hamburger (no bun), a scoop of cottage cheese, and some chunks of pineapple. To this day I associate cottage cheese with dieting and I do not eat it.

Dieting, losing weight, overeating, and then gaining back the weight became the pattern I engaged in for years and years. There wasn't a moment of peace with my body, peace with food, or peace with my weight. Actually, I didn't know that peace with my body was even possible. In college, I began starving myself and overexercising. I remember my college roommate and I dragging ourselves to a dorm mate's room, begging for food. We were caught in a diet/binge/shame cycle that I would continue for years.

Unlike many people I have spoken to, I have not been on every diet imaginable. However, I have tried Weight Watchers (many times), a low-carb diet, the liquid diet, the packaged diet food, and the starvation diet. I even tried being a vegetarian after I read that you can lose weight by not eating meat. I trained for and ran a marathon, thinking it would make me lose weight. Through all of the years and methods, there has never been a diet that allowed me to lose weight and maintain it.

I don't think I ever achieved any of my weight-loss goals on any diet I have tried. That feels sad to say, but it points to my conclusion that diets do not work. I wonder now why I kept at it for so many years. I remember an Oprah story where she lost a significant amount of weight only to start gaining it back the moment she revealed the weight loss. That's me, even though I never met a weight goal. I can temporarily release weight, but then I gain it all back and then some. Shouldn't that have shown me that diets don't work? Instead I bought into the cultural message that if I was not at the perfect weight, I needed to be dieting. If I wasn't at the right weight, I was taught to hate how I looked and tried to change my weight.

I have learned that dieting does not work for me. It makes me obsess about food, obsess about my weight, and obsess about how my body looks. Dieting took up a lot of my time and energy and I still felt unhappy and unsatisfied. When I was losing weight, I felt excited. My happiness was contingent on the number on the scale: I needed to lose enough weight to feel happy. Losing a quarter of a pound was not enough, even though it was something.

There came a time when I was tired of the dieting, tired of my consistent obsession with food, and tired of focusing on my weight. I realized that dieting did not work for me—I was done. It was a simple moment when a small voice inside of me said, "I am done with dieting." I was done feeling scared of food—a simple yet profound message.

I discovered there was a different way to live. This involved changing my behavior, understanding the emotions behind my overeating, managing my thoughts, checking in with my body, and refusing to be upset about my weight. I simply stopped dieting, ate food that nourished my body, and engaged in healthy movement.

First, I changed my behavior. I ditched the diet food that felt restricting. I no longer buy foods that symbolize dieting to me. I have found that diet food varies by individuals, and I decide for myself what feels restricting. Now that I look at food for nourishment rather than for emotional fulfillment, I ask myself, "Will this food give me the energy to do the things I need to do?" If the answer is yes, then I eat it.

Secondly, I looked at my emotions. I found that it is my emotions, more often than not, that lead me to overeat. These emotions are tricky to figure out. I think it is important to notice the feeling first, then acknowledge it. For example, eating once you get home from work when you are feeling lonely or bored and not being able to stop—this is called emotional eating.

Next, I paid attention to my thoughts. What am I telling myself? What derogatory things am I saying to myself? I find that these negative thoughts take me down a road that leads me to overeat. The more positive I am, the less food bugs me, and the less I want to overeat.

Lastly, I examined my ideas about my body. The worse I feel about my body, the more I overeat. It is a cultural phenomenon to feel bad about our bodies, because magazines, television, and movies tell us how we should look. Most of us simply cannot meet these standards, for lots of different reasons.

Now that I've stopped dieting:

- I eat in a way that satisfies my physical hunger.
- I focus on eating when I am hungry and stop when I am full.
- I do not need to own a scale, because I am not obsessed with my weight. I do weigh myself occasionally, but only when I am sure I will not have negative thoughts about my body. I use my clothes and the way my body feels to measure how I am doing.
- I check in with my feelings regularly to see what is going on. I notice the feelings, give them a name, and address them by using a plan to take care of myself.
- I focus on loving who I am now, which includes my body at its currently size.
- I focus on positive thoughts about myself, especially about my body.

I believe that all seemingly negative situations in our lives can be an opportunity for improving ourselves. I can genuinely say I am a better person after looking at my eating issues. I am more self-confident and feel better than ever about myself. And I know that if I can do this, so can you! Take it one step at a time, and I promise you will be happy with the results.

About the Author

Kim McLaughlin has a master's degree in clinical psychology, is a licensed therapist, and a motivational coach who works with people who struggle with dieting and overeating. Her education, experience with clients, as well as her personal history dealing with food, dieting, and weight issues, help her work with people to feel more at peace with food.

Kim wants you to start feeling really good about yourself and your body, as well as assisting you to end your focus on food. She offers group and individual services. She has some special free gifts to help you on your journey at www.FeedYourSoulUnlimited.com/Inspiration.

KEEP TALKING—
DEAD PEOPLE CAN'T TALK!

Wanda King

*"When you know yourself, you are empowered.
When you accept yourself, you are invincible."*

Tina Lifford

November 5, 1976, was a pivotal day that changed the course of my life forever. I graduated high school that summer and couldn't wait for my eighteenth birthday in November so I could finally live out my dream of making my first skydive! The day finally arrived. I jumped out of bed, got dressed, and headed for the local parachute center. I didn't let anyone know where I was going or what I was about to do. This was a personal decision that I felt compelled to do for *me*. On the way, my mind flashed on past memories; it was like a slide show, one after another. One memory, in particular, stood out: I was around twelve years old and knew without a doubt that one day I would fly through the sky under a parachute.

I had always been somewhat of a tomboy growing up; I was never much for playing with Barbies or being a girlie girl. I would rather be playing baseball, riding dirt bikes, and racing go-carts with the boys any day! Often the go-cart races were held next to a small airport that ran a skydiving operation called Falling Stars. It was there I was exposed to the sport of skydiving. In between races, I recalled watching the sky intently as each of the jumper's parachutes opened. I imagined myself like them, flying free as a bird.

And now, here I was! I turned the corner, pulled up to the skydiving center, and parked the car. My heart was beating so fast, it felt as though it was going to pop out of my chest, grow legs, and run as fast as possible in the opposite direction! I don't know if it was because the day was finally here and excitement was filling every breathable space of my body, or if it was fear of the unexpected, that sense of "What the heck am I doing?" I was frozen for a moment as I sat in my car staring at a sign that read "Dunn Airpark, Titusville Parachuting Center." With my heart still pounding like a jackhammer, I instinctively accessed the same strength and courage (or stubbornness!) that had gotten me through many tough times before. I got out of the car and made my way to the office.

It was quiet, and no one seemed to be around. I opened the door to the office, where three men were standing—one behind the counter and two right in front of me. The man behind the counter said, "What do you need, kid?"

I stood tall, mustering every bit of strength and courage I had, and with all eyes staring at me, I said, "I am here to make a skydive!" At that all the tension dissipated, and everyone except for me started to chuckle.

The man then asked, "How old are you?"

"I'm seventeen, but I turn eighteen next Sunday!"

He laughed and told me to come back next Sunday. I looked at those three men and said in a slightly irritated voice, "Oh, I will be back!"

A bit disappointed and perhaps a little relieved, my inner saboteur voice tried to talk me out of pursuing my long-awaited dream. I ignored the voice and was even more determined to show up again on my eighteenth birthday!

The following Sunday, I went back to the skydiving center, determined to realize my dream. Upon arriving, I saw parachutes spread out on the grassy area, ready to be packed for the next jump. People were milling around, talking, and there was an overall sense of high energy. I made my way into the office, encountering the same man that sent me on my way the week before. This time, before he could speak, I announced, "I'm eighteen today, and I want to make a jump!"

He grinned and said, "I didn't think you would be back." He handed me paperwork to complete—waivers, payment information, etc.—and then I completed the required four hours of training with my jumpmaster.

Finally the time came! I suited up and boarded the small plane, making my childhood dream a reality! That moment was everything and more I imagined it would be! For the next ten years, skydiving became my weekend recreation of choice.

Fast-forward to March 1988. Now twenty-nine years old, at a routine doctor's visit, I discovered I had beginning stage cancer cells on the wall of my cervix. The doctor informed me that I would need a complete hysterectomy, and it was scheduled for the following month.

Prior to the surgery I continued to skydive. I began learning another form of the sport called BASE jumping (the acronym BASE stands for Building, Antenna, Span (bridge), and Earth). Instead of jumping from a plane, the jump launches from a stationary object. The risks are much higher than skydiving because BASE jumps are often a thousand feet or less, which doesn't leave any room for error. I first started BASE jumping with a group of experienced friends, where I learned to jump from an 1,150-foot antenna tower. The experience was intense, crazy, and scary—all at once!

A couple of weeks after the doctor's visit, friends asked me to meet them at the local river to participate in a jump never attempted before by anyone. After arriving, my friends explained the following details to me: The person is lifted 200 feet via a parasail towed by a boat. At 200 feet, the person detaches from the parasail, begins falling, immediately deploys a packed parachute he is wearing, and glides safely in the water! It sounded like fun to me!

My two friends went first; everything worked perfectly. Both of them landed safely in the water. However, when it was my turn, the landing was very different than my friends' landings. When the parasail reached 200 feet, I released the connected parasail, threw out the pilot chute used to deploy the main parachute, and . . . *nothing happened.* The main parachute did not open! I impacted the water at 80 to 90 mph. At the moment of impact, a loud voice from within screamed, NOOOO! OPEN YOUR EYES AND CLOSE YOUR MOUTH! My response was simultaneous to the command, and I went underwater with eyes open and mouth shut. Doctors later informed me that this contributed to saving my life.

My friends acted quickly, lifting me from the water using a boogie board, and the ambulance rushed me to the local hospital. I sensed I was in critical condition and fought to hold onto life. My prognosis showed multiple vertebrae fractures (including spinal cord damage resulting in paralysis below my chest), left and right kidneys damaged from impact, and internal bleeding.

Soon after arriving at the hospital, I began hearing the same inner voice that screamed earlier when I hit the water. The voice now chanted, "KEEP TALKING—DEAD PEOPLE CAN'T TALK" over and over. With whatever strength I had, I began to speak. I'm sure the words I spoke made no sense, but the bottom line was that, while words were coming from my mouth, I was still alive. For what seemed like hours, the voice kept chanting those same words.

Later that evening I was airlifted to an advanced hospital better equipped to handle the extent of my injuries. During one of four surgeries, I coded on the operating table, but the team resuscitated me and brought me back to life. I spent the next three months in the hospital's spinal unit. After being upgraded from intensive care to progressive care, I had an out-of-body experience. As I was looking down at my listless body lying in the bed, I could run and jump everywhere. When I returned to my body, I knew I would not be paralyzed for long and would walk out of that hospital. And sure enough, a few weeks into my stay, I began to have slight movement in my toes and gradually in my legs!

One day, as the chaos settled and I was able to start sorting out my new world, it occurred to me that I had never had the scheduled hysterectomy. I informed one of the nurses of the situation, and an OB/GYN doctor was contacted from the hospital to use a new procedural technique that removes the cancerous cells from the cervix instead of performing a complete hysterectomy. The downside was little hope of ever having a successful pregnancy. The surgery was a success, all cancer was removed, and soon I would be discharged from the hospital after spending three long months.

The Impossible Means I'm Possible

The day I was discharged, I walked out of the hospital on my own. Several months later I went skydiving with friends, and one year after my accident, I delivered my miracle: an eight-pound, fifteen-ounce healthy baby girl! Four years later I became a competitive bodybuilder, placing in the top rank of my class. I am married to my best friend, I enjoy riding my Harley, and I'm helping my daughter plan her wedding! Life is amazing!

And all because of a twelve-year-old girl's dream! You may be thinking, *Dream? You almost died!* But that experience was priceless; because of it, I now have a beautiful daughter and the unspeakable joy she has given me for the last twenty-seven years. I have learned the value of all life, and I've been given a second chance to make a difference in the lives of others!

If you dream it, you can do it! Allow your strength and your Inspired Self to be your guide!

About the Author

Wanda King, the founder of Discover Clear Vision, is a business owner, business coach, speaker, author, and learning and development expert. She is familiar personally and professionally with the adverse experiences and the inner saboteur messages women are faced with every day. Through her many life experiences, Wanda rediscovered her self-worth and reclaimed her inner "Goddess Warrior," and she now has a passion to share it with the world! She developed a deep self-awareness in knowing that self-worth and inner strength are never taken or lost, but freely given away by allowing other people or things to control one's joy and success.

Wanda is passionate about her purpose in helping and supporting others to communicate their value through her coaching skills and training. She offers proven techniques and strategies that empower her clients to defeat their "inner saboteur voice" and shift into their "inspired self voice" so they can communicate their self-worth from the inside out!

Visit her online now at WWW.DiscoverClearVision.com.

DAMAGED GOODS

Suzi Fox

"Life is 10 percent what happens to you and 90 percent how you react to it."
                                                  Charles R. Swindoll

As I was growing up in the Midwest, when someone referred to a girl with a past no one wanted to talk about, they would say she was "damaged goods." They usually referred to her as someone who "got around," someone who had been indiscreet with the boys. When I got older the term was used in reference to girls who "had issues"—as if they were mentally impaired. The inference was that girls like this were not worth getting to know, so others should keep their distance.

I often wondered why this term was only used in reference to women. Not once did I hear it describing a male. Why were we women considered a bad investment of time or affection just because we had hit

Damaged Goods

a bump while navigating the relationship road? Why were we talked about as if we were packaged meat, and "they" (whoever *they* were) got to decide if we were good enough to be prime choice or tossed into the about-to-be-spoiled section? It didn't take me long to learn that life was not merciful—if a female became a damsel in distress, it was her own fault and others were better off staying away. After all, a man wouldn't want her reputation to ruin his, now would he?

People don't get damaged all by themselves. It usually takes at least one other participant to contribute to the demise of one's healthy choices. So I ask you this: Were you ever looked at as damaged goods? If you have ever been molested, mistreated, taken advantage of, abused, or manipulated, then you're in the running. If you have ever been cheated on, beaten up, deceived by others, or kicked to the curb, let me officially welcome you to the Damaged Goods Group. This is not a committee; those on a committee get to choose that position, while the Damaged Goods Group usually has that title bestowed upon them when they're not looking. The Damaged Goods Group is not a club either—if it were a club, that would have meant we had been trying really hard to qualify for membership.

The Damaged Goods Group is a global gathering of girls who have been set up and beat up, yet we continue to step up into the ring (with or without our boxing gloves) in order to hash out another day. We have had people play tricks on us, hoping to incite us to anger so they could further prove how superior they were to us. But instead of assuming the fetal position (as we may have in the beginning), we swallow our pride and refuse to be denied access to a life of empowerment. We are mothers to our children, we are mistresses to our husbands, and we are entrepreneurs. We are bank presidents and CEOs of billion-dollar corporations. After decades of abuse, we are proving to the world that we are not damaged—but we are dangerous. We are a threat to those who think they are safe from the scorn and scrutiny of others. We may have been messed up for a season, but now we are determined not to miss out on the best of what life has to offer.

At one time we were manipulated by fear; now we are fearless. We have tasted death, and now we know death has no sting so we charge into its face, completely unafraid of how others look at us. What was meant for our demise has become fuel for our message. What was intended to strike pain into our hearts has morphed into compassion—our calling card to gather those around the globe who have experienced similar setbacks.

Our weapons are resilience, strength, and persistence. We believe in second chances. We promote our sisters who have struggled and wept over lost opportunities, and we throw them a lifeline called hope. We may have been knocked down hundreds of times, but we know the only option is to get up one more time.

Damaged Goods

We may have been alone in our own battles, but now we seek out others to encourage them in their progress.

To those who would judge, convict, and condemn us, we are your biggest enemy. Why? Because we don't care what you think. We have already been to hell and back. We know the path well, and we know how to get out of deep, dark holes of depression. We know how to feed a family of five a three-course meal on less than five dollars and be grateful for it. We know how to create business plans from an idea that sprung from a dream that woke us up at 3:00 a.m. We know how to take the ashes of a relationship we thought would last forever . . . and create art.

The only thing damaged is your view of who we were all along on the inside. Those who mistreated us never could have imagined who we would become. They tried to make us victims, and instead we are victorious. We do not seek any trophies; instead we strive to bring others clarity from confusion.

If you have ever found yourself in the damaged goods gully, you know the only way out is by choice. We forgive because we must. We let go of torment so we don't get tricked. We don't grip the past, hoping for payback time; instead we align with faith for a better future. Those who may have caused pain in our lives are no longer considered our enemies; we view them as our teachers. They have gifted us with rich life experiences that have strengthened our souls and provided perspective for our empowerment.

We were never damaged goods at all; it was only someone's twisted perspective of who they wanted us to be. Perhaps the fires of conflict heated up those creative gifts that needed to come forth all along. Or maybe it was the press of contention that squeezed the juice within that poured forth the drink of a life worth living. These distractions may have caused a sequence of events that gave us options in life. When we choose the higher road, those decisions lead to a destiny beyond what anyone could have ever imagined!

If you are a photographer, point your lens to what you want your focus to be. If you are a dancer, this is your opening night—revel in it, bloody toes and all! If you are a business owner, this is your grand opening for a wonderful new journey into prosperity. If you are a mom, you are about to give birth to a child who will change the world forever. You are a person who has been placed on this planet at this point in time with a purpose and a plan like no other. Only you can do what you do the way you do it. You have a passion burning inside of you and a mission to let the multitudes know. If you don't, the world will suffer the loss of your contribution. So you see, you aren't damaged goods now, and you never have been. Your mess was meant to be a message all along. This talent and power resided in you since the beginning of time. There is nothing left to be afraid of; there is only adventure! Embrace the challenges—they will always provide fuel for a great future.

About the Author

Suzi Fox, originally from Chicago, is an engaging author whose work is not only entertaining but enables readers to see their own challenges with a new perspective of hope and a fresh commitment to enjoy the process. Her life's mission is to encourage, educate, and empower others to live vibrant and fulfilled lives. Suzi is a mother of three, resides in Southern California, and enjoys international travel, days at the beach, boogie boarding, cycling, and hiking. She is the author of Travel Tips with Toddlers, a business owner, and a sought-after public speaker and trainer. You can view her blogs and contact her through GlueYourLifeBackToBetter.com.

CHILDHOOD DREAMS INSPIRE GROWN-UP SERVICE

Kathy Pendleton

> *"Never go to a doctor whose office plants have died."*
>
> **Erma Bombeck**

What has inspired an idea in you? What has inspired you to take action on an idea? Was it part of a childhood dream? For me, as a child I wanted to become a doctor. It was an idea that seemed to have always been there. Now, morphed by years and experiences, this interest in medical service has taken hold again. How did that happen? That's the story of my inspiration!

I abandoned the idea of becoming a doctor at the suggestion of my parents. Instead, I enjoyed a good career in computer technology, and it provided opportunities for travel and fun and exposure to many ideas and experiences I would never have encountered otherwise. Along the way I discovered that I have a gift for teaching, for breaking down complex subjects into simple steps, for arranging topics in an order that has students asking for the next subject.

My favorite job brought me a mentor who was wildly passionate about her life as a nurse and owner of a home health agency. She rekindled my interest in the medical field as we discussed how patients experience their medical care. I saw the need for patients and their families to obtain the information necessary to make important decisions about care, treatment, life, and death. This mentor was passionate about the care of patients, and it was contagious. But while I was interested, I wasn't inspired to do anything about it because I was already involved in my chosen field.

Many years passed, and I left my technology career, feeling the need to make more of a contribution. About this same time, my seventy-year-old mother-in-law had back surgery, and I went to help. When she arrived at her hospital room after the surgery, she was suffering from severe pain. I asked the nurses for pain medication, believing it would arrive soon. It didn't. I returned to the nurses' station several times, asking again and again. Eventually I became angry with the nurses who were answering me but not delivering any pain medication. I ended up shouting at them, but still no pain medication came.

Her suffering finally overcame my anger and my fear that she and my father-in-law would think me crazy.

I whispered into her ear to follow me to a place of warmth and safety and no pain, a sunny beach with hot breezes, waves lapping, and a happy, loving family laughing together. She eventually relaxed and went to sleep. My father-in-law was amazed—and actually so was I. In those moments, I had truly been inspired to step outside my own fears in the service of someone else. I can still remember the wondrous calm and immense gratitude that her pain relief was delivered through me.

Still determined to find out why the pain medication took hours to show up, I asked a friend, a hospital pharmacist, about the situation, and she answered without missing a beat, "Oh, the doctor never ordered it." I was horrified. Even if he forgot and went into another surgery, there must have been some way for her nurses to get it. They never told me about the error, and they didn't take steps to get it on their own. I was indignant that the nurses would allow a patient to suffer that level of pain without finding a way to help her.

I was inspired to make a difference and determined to figure out how I could get the information I needed to understand how the hospital system of nurses and doctors and patients worked. A few years later, my father-in-law was hospitalized with his third bout of a MRSA staph infection. By the time it was discovered, he was given a fifty-fifty chance of surviving. Eventually it was my turn to help my mother-in-law. Sitting in the hospital room daily, I observed what went on around me. Things were happening that concerned me, but I didn't know how to work the system.

I called all of my friends who had anything to do with medicine and asked questions. Many other friends had elderly parents with medical issues, so I also gleaned lots of good information from their perspectives. I found myself energized by my increased understanding of what was going on. When my father-in-law had a small stroke on a Saturday morning, I was appalled that there seemed to be nothing happening to help him. I thought about it, decided on a course of action, and within a short time his doctor brought a neurologist to the hospital room. The next day I mentioned to this same doctor that no respiratory therapist had come the day before to verify his ability to swallow. The doctor got the therapist into the room very quickly.

I had made a difference in the level of care he received! I found myself inspired to ask questions, pay more attention, understand the process, and occasionally create a change. Friends continued to share their stories about themselves or their family members, and the more stories I heard, the more obvious it became that they were having the same frustrating experiences I was—and more. There *had* to be a better way, and I would persist until I found it!

But, boy, was I . . . *angry*! I wanted others to benefit from what I had learned, and it wasn't working. I was inspired by my experiences, but when I told other people these stories, my anger seeped out—probably *streamed* out—and those around me weren't interested. In the end, the people I wanted to help just wanted to get away from me.

Because of my desire to connect with people and encourage them to participate in their own and their families' healthcare treatment and decisions, I worked to transform my anger into compassion and concern. It required years of reflection, years of examining my own motivation. Was I just out to get even in some sense? Friends and coaches helped by encouraging me to continue. Their assurances that I was slowly changing kept me going.

I kept plugging away—asking questions, talking about my experiences, reading books about other patients' and families' experiences. I worked with coaches and trainers to create speeches that would create connection rather than distance. And very slowly, my love of family and desire to be of service overtook the anger and softened into the compassion needed for healing.

These days my inspiration burns brighter than ever. When someone asks what I do, I tell them I teach people to be medical spokespersons for their families, and the stories pour out. The stories are all different, and yet all of them demonstrate love and caring, the understanding and awareness that intimacy within families brings. The knowledge a mom has of her child or

Childhood Dreams Inspire Grown-up Service

a husband has of his wife is not the same as medical expertise, but it is just as important, just as valid. I'm inspired to reassure family members that their observations are important and contribute to the understanding the experts are building for a patient. When other people tell me that this is important, I'm inspired to continue, and I believe that my willingness to ask questions and poke my nose in where I'm not invited are good things.

This inspiration came to me late in life and has been created by my life experiences. My willingness to accept it fanned its flame. It has become a driving force. My wish for you is that when something inspires you, see where it leads. Accept it and nurture it. In turn, your inspiration will nurture you and bring you more connection and fulfillment than you could ever imagine.

About the Author

Kathy Pendleton grew up in Virginia, attended college in the East, and gave up her childhood dreams for a more pragmatic career in computer technology. Her strengths in analyzing, simplifying, and teaching complex computer processes led her to fulfill dreams of travel, experiencing life outside the USA, and appreciation for many varying points of view. She uses these strengths today to teach people to speak up and be the patient advocate for their family members. She is a best-selling author and speaker. Kathy lives in Tahoe City, California with her husband, Tom.

HEAL YOURSELF—
FREE YOUR SOUL

Sasha Sabbeth

When you follow your bliss, doors will open where you would not have thought there would be doors; and where there wouldn't be a door for anyone else.

Joseph Campbell

I am three years old. It's nighttime. My bedroom is dark and the door is closed. I stand up in my crib and begin screaming. A nonphysical being is standing in the middle of my room. He is saying, "You will never be happy in this lifetime. You may think you are happy. But no matter how much you try, I will never let you be happy in this life." My mother comes in and soothes me.

I am six years old. Again I wake up in the middle of the night. I have an insistent sugar craving for ice cream, pastries, pies. I get out of bed and quietly go into the garage. I open the family freezer, take out a quart of ice

> cream, and eat the entire carton. I feel guilty, relieved, ashamed, afraid, and relaxed all at once. I repeat this every few days until my mother puts a lock on the freezer to prevent me from doing this again. She tells me to wake her up when I have that overwhelming desire for sugar. I never wake her up the next time it happens, though. When I feel the craving again, I go to the refrigerator instead and eat whatever I can find.

From the time I was in elementary school, I experienced severe constipation. I tried and tried to have a bowel movement, but nothing happened. I remember feeling bloated and uncomfortable for days at a time. My mother took me to a colonic therapist who prescribed enemas and laxatives, which I used every few days. This evolved into a lifestyle of mandatory daily routines until my late thirties when I discovered the cause of my constipation problems.

I also suffered with recurring boils and bacterial and virile infections that resulted in breakouts on my lower torso, thighs, and feet. Chronic canker sores made it painful to brush my teeth. I experienced frightening asthma attacks frequently. I often woke up in the morning panicked and crying because my eyes were sealed shut with mucous excretions that glued my eyelashes shut. My body was my enemy.

I knew my parents loved me, yet a chronic emotional anguish nagged at me. I felt lonely, insecure, and lost most of the time. At school I was often bullied and shunned, leaving me humiliated, shamed, and shocked.

In junior high my theater arts talents—singing, dancing, acting—blossomed. I was often cast in lead roles of musicals and dramas at camp, school, and our Jewish temple productions. These successes momentarily distracted me from my otherwise subterranean pain and emotional chaos. My performance talents led to my decision to leave New York and attend a university in Canada as a Theater Arts major.

Glimmers of hope, acceptance, loving friendships, successful creative projects, and a sense of belonging gradually began to take root in my life. I wrote and delivered a children's musical as a drama counselor at a summer camp. I discovered an otherworldly inner realm that sourced and fueled my creativity. Shiatsu acupressure treatments healed my childhood asthma.

My other health matters persisted, however. My bloated abdomen caused me to have the constant appearance of being two or three months pregnant. Finally I could no longer function or ignore my unresolved health symptoms. I dropped out of university and returned to New York. I spiraled into despair—what kind of future would I have? I was terrified.

Then God sent me a rescuer: I met a man who mentally and emotionally saved my life. A brilliant musician, he became my first spiritual teacher. For the next several years, he indoctrinated me into the world of psychic intuitive realms, meditation, and the transformational power of music. This formed a reference point I would later revisit when I discovered my own power as a Sound Healer.

Signs began to appear. At one point, I attended a class that promised participants to consciously connect with our guardian angels. During a private reading with the teacher, she told me, "You were born to be a healer. You will impact masses of people with your healing vocal tones."

I went to a psychic energy healer in my relentless search to heal my health issues. In our first session together, he said, "Please show me the palms of your hands." He looked at my outstretched hands. It was as if he was seeing through me. He said, "You know, you were born to be a healer. You have powerful healing hands and clairvoyant sight. I suggest that you practice feeling and sensing peoples' auras."

Impossible, I thought. *How could I be a healer given my own problems?*

My purpose became unmistakable in ways I simply could not deny. I decided to become a paralegal student, wanting to have a specialized career. One day, I was studying with a fellow student at her home. She was a performance opera singer. I told her about my healer's recommendation that I practice reading peoples' auras, and she agreed to be my guinea pig.

I began moving my hands around her energy field. I heard a strong male voice inside my head telling me,

"Sing!" I was shaken to hear a voice instructing me with such forceful command, and I felt too insecure to sing in the presence of a professional. When I did not respond to his directive, I heard the voice again with even more force: "Sing!" I was now more afraid *not* to follow "orders." I opened my mouth, and out came otherworldly, flutelike, crystal-bowl-sounding vocal tones. My friend immediately became deeply relaxed. She began to see visions of angels and scenes of other eras dance on the screen of her mind. She sensed that she was seeing past life flashbacks. She was in awe of her response to my sounds and deeply moved emotionally by the purity of my tones.

My communication with the spirit realm further unfolded when I worked with a New Age musician to create a recording that would become a healing meditation product. I asked him to create synthesizer wind and bell tracks to which I would then add my vocals. He agreed, and we met late one night after midnight in his non-soundproof studio so that his kids, wife, and pets would be asleep.

> *He plays his prerecorded synthesizer track once for me. As I listen, I go into a trance. When he plays the track a second time, I see a series of spirits float into the room. The energy in the studio becomes peaceful with a regal and loving ambiance. A spirit places a crystal in my aura at my third eye and another crystal at my heart*

> chakra. I ask the musician to play the synthesizer track again. I open my mouth. An effortless stream of tones in perfect harmony with his soundtrack flow out of me. No edits are needed. The result was my meditation and healing recording, Sacred Peace.

I moved to Colorado and then to California. I was still seeking solutions for my health issues. I was also searching for the appropriate scenarios to position myself as a spiritual guide who provides healing with sound and energy transmissions. I appeared on cable TV and several radio shows. I was a presenter at various holistic and humanist conferences. On a practical level, I was self-employed because I was not employable: My unpredictable health episodes prevented me from keeping consistent work schedules for an employer. I could not produce high-quality work on a reliable basis. I was frequently fired. Being self-employed allowed me to work my schedule around my health challenges. I became confident that I could earn a living offering the same modalities with clients as I was implementing on myself. I launched my business with a palate of services. As a certified hypnotherapist, neurolinguistic programmer, masseuse, acupressurist, Reiki master, and success coach, I witnessed my clients' and students' transformation. Lifelong sabotaging behaviors and emotions were replaced with confidence, creative innovation, and happiness. I wrote and taught a course entitled *Life Purpose*.

My nonstop search for health solutions finally revealed my need for digestive enzymes and intestinal support flora via probiotics. At last, my elimination issues were resolved! The healing of my aching emotional heart happened when I became the adopted mother of a fur child, my former fiance's dog, a pit bull named Echo.

Through my path of self-healing, I discovered my soul. My international business offers the types of services that finally brought me to a flourishing, prosperous, and functional life using three distinct components. I have clustered these components into a self-healing system for personal and professional success: *The Spiritual Power Success Essentials: Psychic Intuition Skills, Energy Healing Management, and Soul Purpose Clarity.*

I was inspired to never give up, to keep searching for solutions, and to develop my life vision in order to freely express my God-given talents in ways that uplift humanity. If you are struggling with layers of relentless obstacles, I offer you a magic-wand formula that has become my signature message: Partner with your spirit realm, fixate on your purpose, and design a destiny to "Succeed In Sync With Your Soul."

About the Author

Sasha Sabbeth is internationally recognized as a Soul Purpose expert, Master Sound and Energy Healer, emerging public speaker, Spiritual Business Coach, and the Entrepreneur's Intuition and Purpose Soul Coach Healer. With thirty years of experience, she facilitates her clients, students, and audiences in removing blocks to their success, accelerating intuition access, claiming a deeper embodiment of their Soul Purpose, and igniting their creative genius for soul-sourced solutions. She does this by implementing her *Divine Triad Toolkit*: a customized personal and business mentoring system where she activates broadcasted Divine energy called *The Transmissions of Grace, Celestial Toning Sound Healing*, and *Intuitive Energy Scan Readings*. Her message is: Succeed In Sync With Your Soul. Her mission is to Heal the Heart of Humanity through mentoring Soul Purpose-guided business owners and through the reverent honoring of our Other Species brethren. Sasha is also an animal healer and intuitive.

Sasha is trained as a Reiki Master, Soma Pi Energy Healer, Hypnotherapist, Neuro-Linguistic Programmer, Certified Print Personality Profile Coach, True Purpose Coach, Passion Test Facilitator, and has studied various forms of intuition, energy healing, and empowerment success coaching systems.

http://www.entrepreneursoulcoach.com
sasha@entrepreneursoulcoach.com

How Good Can Emerge From The Bad

Sheryl Hensel

"We delight in the beauty of the butterfly, but rarely admit the changes it has gone through to achieve that beauty."

Maya Angelou

There are times in life when we think we're in control, only to learn that we really are not. When we look deep within at what lessons can be learned from all events we experience in life, it can help lessen the pain—or not. The choice is ours. It may take time for the true lesson to come forth, but it will if we expect it. We can find the blessing in all events, fortunate and unfortunate. I promise you that when gratitude is expressed, the path becomes lighter. I hope my story may inspire you to look for the possibilities of good that can emerge from the bad.

How Good Can Emerge from the Bad

I began my career as a middle school teacher, because I was drawn to working with children and helping them learn. I became the student council advisor, coached multiple sports, and was on top of my game. When I was promoted to a new position as the district-wide School-to-Work coordinator, I fell in love with education all over again.

My path, however, took a totally new direction two years later in 1998. Leaving a work conference and heading to buy some classroom supplies, I was waiting at a stoplight and witnessed a motorist in distress. Her car veered across four lanes of traffic, and I could see that she slumped over sideways as the car continued moving. Eventually the car stopped on the sidewalk, and I knew whatever was happening was bad. I rushed to assist the driver, and moments later while speaking with 911, I was struck by another motorist. In the end, I was the only one taken to the hospital; I sustained a severe closed head injury and brain trauma. The driver of the first car had had a seizure and refused treatment. She was not even supposed to be driving—her license had been suspended due to her condition.

I didn't notice any brain damage until about six months after the accident. The first sign that something wasn't right was when I began experiencing migraine headaches. Despite nine months of extensive rehabilitation and Western medicine appointments, I continued to suffer from migraines, limited cognitive functioning, general pain, and depression. The hardest part of it all was that I "looked" okay, but things weren't clicking inside. It was frustrating to know I wasn't remembering things like I used to, while visibly appearing just fine. It wasn't like having a broken leg in a cast, obvious to others that you are injured. My family and friends didn't understand what was wrong with me, and that compounded the situation. It took me years to understand what a blessing that accident was to me.

At the time, I didn't give thanks for the accident even though at some level I *knew* I was lucky it happened. The morning after the accident, I was at home and got a call to come into work if at all possible. A student brought a gun to school and shot himself at his locker just minutes before classes started. I would have been one of the first teachers on scene as the young man's locker was not too far from my classroom. That accident spared me the horrific memories I'm sure I would have had. God knew that was one experience I didn't need to carry throughout my life. It wasn't until years later, however, that I realized how divine things really are.

Another blessing that came from the accident was the motivation to move out of Michigan due to the migraines. Doctors told me the barometric changes were too much for my brain and I needed to move to a steady climate. Moving to Florida allowed me the opportunity to be an administrator, this time in charge of adults.

How Good Can Emerge from the Bad

This experience taught me so much about youth struggling with life, adults struggling with their demons, and my shortcomings as a supervisor. That job just wasn't my cup of tea, but I'm grateful for the experience.

The next blessing of the accident was discovering Quantum Energetics Structured Therapy (QEST). This noninvasive treatment healed my "brain fog." It impressed me so much that I decided to become a QEST practitioner. The curriculum was more difficult than any class I'd taken in college, yet it excited and inspired me. Never in my wildest dreams did I think I'd be living in Florida and flying back and forth to Colorado for two years to learn a form of healing work.

Living in Florida exposed me to the spiritual world and taught me how to learn from nature. I was blessed with some wonderful friends, clients, and a new family due to the accident. The winding spiritual path of self-discovery was part of my healing process. Learning to go within to help my body heal and then teach others to do the same is one of the greatest gifts the accident gave me. I know through my experiences that it is possible for one's body to heal on its own. Someday I believe we will teach our children how to do this so doctors and medication can truly be for emergencies.

After a short-term move to Denver, my final move—up to this point!—was to Southern California, where I *never* thought I would live. I remember as a young girl saying, "I wish I could live somewhere that it was 70–80 degrees all year. Does that place exist?" The response was always, "Yes, Southern California." I laugh when I think of that because I had the image of California being too expensive and never thought I could afford living there. Yet I envisioned it at a very young age. That's the power of our words and minds!

The point of this little journey around the country is that, through all of my trials and tribulations, I learned to go with the flow. We can't imagine what great things are in store for us because we only know what we know. When we limit our thinking to the here-and-now, we take away from what could be. I can't say every step of the way has been easy, but I kept going. I started over several times and moved to areas where I didn't know a soul. I moved to Newport Beach and started a new business within a month of moving to California. I didn't have an email list, previous client list to pull from, or a single person to help me maneuver everything. I just jumped in and figured it out.

My final blessing from the accident is being able to work with people in groups or individually, teaching them how they can heal their bodies. As America's Brain Injury Awareness Advocate, educating people that they may have had a brain injury is just the beginning of assisting them to a deeper self-awareness and appreciation of life.

When you have faith, you have faith. It shouldn't be something that is conditional or situational. When you *truly* believe that everything works out as it is meant to, life becomes much less stressful. You are able to enjoy the ride and trust that a higher power is truly in charge. Even if there are detours, one way or another you will be led back to your true path. Maybe, like me, it will happen through a head injury. The sooner you discover your inspiration, the sooner you will receive the abundance the universe has waiting for you.

Sheryl Hensel

About the Author

Sheryl Hensel is America's Brain Injury Awareness Advocate and author of *Your Amazing Itty Bitty Concussion Book: 15 Vital Things You Need to Know About Brain Injuries*. Her discussion regarding brain injuries appeal to those who have been concussed, the brain-injured, and caregivers.

As a previous teacher, school administrator, day-treatment center principal, and entrepreneur, Sheryl has a wealth of experiences to teach/guide people through their personal healing journey. Most importantly, she suffered a brain injury that led to nine months of cognitive rehabilitation and a disability leave from teaching.

Sheryl has come full circle as a student, teacher, administrator, healer, and survivor and is able to provide relative information to all levels of brain injuries.

THE POWER OF GIVING

Jason Robins

The more difficulties one has to encounter, within and without, the more significant and the higher in inspiration his life will be.

Horace Bushnell

When I was a young boy, I had a driving force that was selfless and deep. I felt strongly that there must be justice for the plants, the birds, the bees, and the trees. Where did this come from? I'm not sure, but it was a powerful sense of compassion for the earth with all its animals and beings. It was a passion, a calling, that would not be fully realized until later in life. Like many, I wanted to save the world, but from what?

When I was in grade school, I was so impassioned about the destruction of the rain forest and ongoing environmental degradation that I decided that I had to do something. As a representative in my student government, I brought up the idea of hosting a book sale at the school to raise money to save the rain forest. The project involved getting parents to donate used and unwanted books to the cause. Then we would sell those books right back to the parents. The idea worked well enough to save twenty-five acres for a few years. That was a big success for someone so young.

It took me a long time to realize that the world needed saving from *us*. Human beings are consuming resources faster than natural cycles and biospheres can replenish. The selfless and compassionate Jason soon became cynical about the direction society was headed, but I never stopped to question this attitude. It was an attitude of self-importance. The young self that was so passionate about helping people and saving the environment from human-caused degradation would remain lost for at least a decade. This is the story of how I began to live my life in a new way—how my thoughts and concerns changed from *me* to *us*.

During college, I found myself upset about having to work community service hours. I could no longer justify giving time and energy away to a cause for free. I had no real concern for anyone but myself. I had become one of the mindless consumers only concerned with my own well-being. Upon graduating I felt lost; I had no purpose and no drive to do anything. I lacked direction. I was in a sinkhole that seemed relentless and unescapable. I was merely going through the motions. But over the next couple of years, something big was about to happen.

Jason Robins

I began volunteering for an environmental green non-profit called the Sustainable Business Council of Los Angeles. I thought I had touched base with my roots and found my calling: to be an environmentalist. But how does one become an environmentalist? I felt passionate about the issues, but I lacked the necessary knowledge and skills. Did I have the drive to accomplish something bigger than myself? Certainly not at first—that would take a few more years. That wouldn't happen until I started to change my understanding about earning and its connection to giving. Anyone can make a product and sell it and even become a millionaire, but how are they affecting the earth and society? My goal was to do something profoundly different than the status quo.

I was employed by Environment California as a paid "beggar." We were sharing the message and educating people, but we were also asking for money all day, every day. I was not good at asking people to give money. I really cared about the issues but I questioned, was this the best way to do something about them? Were all these charities really making a difference? Were they saving the world, or were they just bogged down by raising money? Had the activists and lobbyists for these nonprofits been corrupted over time? Did they have a real passion for the issues, or just the experience and knowledge to get it done?

Some of us give so much that we find ourselves flat broke, penniless, and dependent upon others. We almost become our own charity—but what if giving could be both profitable *and* charitable? I believe it can be. Toms' one-for-one program is one example. This small company has grown and is an inspiration to many young, up-and-coming entrepreneurs.

I began a new venture with a business partner: we started a credit card processing sales organization, Loyalty Processing. Our goal was to provide a more personalized service and look out for the best interests of the merchants, not the banks and processors. We wanted to be a trusted resource and develop long-term business relationships with honest businesspeople. But my partner and I found that this wasn't enough. Not everyone understood what they were paying, and trust did not come easy from those we were hoping to serve. I began to get discouraged.

I joined a local networking group called BNI, the largest referral organization, which promotes reciprocity. As you build relationships with people in your community, you build your reputation and your brand equity. Devoting time to search for referrals and looking out and listening for referrals for your colleagues makes you indispensable. Being selfish and not acting with abundance leaves you empty inside and also harms your business.

But then I realized again that we have to stop waiting for others to save the world. We have to do our part by giving. How could I incorporate giving into my business, Loyalty Processing? My partner and I began working with 1% for the Planet, and now 1 percent of our revenues go to charities that focus on saving and conserving the environment.

My new belief is that all kinds of giving can make us more successful and help us enjoy a more fulfilling life purpose. Giving in the form of time volunteered, money, or material goods can really make a difference how people perceive you. By reinventing myself this way, I brought renewed meaning and purpose back into Loyalty Processing, business and life. Giving referrals to fellow colleagues and friends so they can build their business helps build mine. Giving builds relationships, and this helps market your business to people with common values who want to consume your products or services. I am sure that as I grow as a person and my company continues to grow, giving will continue to be an integral part of what I do. My hope is that this will also inspire our clients to give. Incorporating giving into your business can make a big difference in the "bottom line" of your company. The law of reciprocity always applies. I suggest you get started!

About the Author

Jason Robins is a managing director at Loyalty Processing and gladly supports 1% for the Planet by donating 1 percent of revenues to them. Jason is passionate about saving the environment, hiking, climbing, and any outdoor activity. He is also passionate about reducing the fees his clients pay on their merchant processing. When he's not climbing Mt. Whitney, attending Burning Man, or working with clients, Jason likes to volunteer with organizations that help preserve our parklands and protect our natural resources. He earned his BA in politics from UC Santa Cruz. You can visit him at www.LoyaltyProcessing.com.

BLESSING IN DISGUISE

Jennifer Darling

"The greater part of our happiness or misery depends upon our dispositions, and not upon our circumstances."

Martha Washington

When I first launched my business, my husband, parents, family, mentors, and friends all played an integral part in my motivation on a daily basis. However, there was one inspiring person who truly pushed me over the edge—one person without whom I would not have taken the giant leap into entrepreneurship. It was not immediately apparent to me that this person was the major contributor to my success; in fact, the opposite seemed true—I suffered under his management for years. What I realize today, though, is that the biggest blessing I have ever received was working for this former boss. He taught me, through many trials, that I am strong, smart, and good enough to accomplish what I set out to do. I believe this is true for many of you, too. As I started sharing my experience, I heard countless women tell me a similar story. They are still too deep in the fog of anxiety and stress to see the way out. They are unable to see their situation as a blessing in disguise yet. They feel stuck.

If you feel this way, you must know that what you are experiencing is a gift. You become free from anxiety when you open your mind to the possibility of the greatness of this gift. You have a choice, and even if that choice is not immediately evident, it is there if you listen. In my case, I thought I was not good enough. I believed it would be a sign of weakness if I gave up and quit my job. Instead, I plowed through a bad situation until I was mentally exhausted and physically sick.

The Situation

From the minute I walked through the door of my new job, I sensed that something was amiss. The promises made to me during the interview process had vanished for various reasons out of my boss's control. The beautiful picture painted of the income potential, autonomy, and support system was not reality. My boss treated me poorly and gave me opposing direction every other week. Do this; no, do that; no, change this; now change that. He encouraged my staff to complain about me, and he used the information against me. I was in a no-win situation, but I was determined to stick it out and figure out a way to make it work. I was resolved to find a way to have everyone like me. My first-year employee feedback remarks were lackluster, but by the second year, I had turned things around and was gelling with the team.

My team's sales were in the tank the first year, but I found a way out of that, too, and achieved my budgets. It was not good enough, however. I successfully launched a massive sales campaign and was reprimanded for taking responsibility on my own. But then I was rewarded for my accomplishment. I entered into another round of conflicting communication. The internal politics and drama were too much. The micromanagement increased. My ideas were stolen and credited to others. I had never been so confused about my job priorities in my life.

The temperature rose every year. Then there was the bullying; the passive-aggressive threats; the implications to upper management that I wasn't good enough. One year my team made our budgets and I received the highest leadership scores, yet my annual review was unsatisfactory. When I asked what I could have done differently, the reply was that I didn't support the support staff. My team was pitted against every other team; accounts were continuously taken from us and not returned. Somehow even though our performance was above all the other teams, I felt like a failure.

The Breaking Point

I took personality tests and career placement tests to determine if this was the right fit. I read personal development books to try to figure out what was wrong with me. I earned a master's degree in management. I complained to my friends about my situation. When I got tired of annoying my friends, I sought professional counseling. At least the counselor was paid to listen to my woes. I was depressed, I suffered from panic attacks, and had started taking antianxiety medication.

I was physically ill, too. I was suffering from asthma, allergies, and had developed a chronic cough. In one year, I visited the doctor over fifty times! During one annual review, my boss's boss told me that my cough was a distraction to the workflow and was likely why the other employees claimed they work in an unhealthy and unsafe work environment. That was it! I cried all the way to my therapist's office, who was appalled. I began visiting specialists and undergoing rigorous medical tests, and the final diagnosis was stress. When my doctor told me I had to quit my job or I would die, I made an exit plan for myself. Without a new job to go to, I created my own.

The Lesson

I realized that I was a victim—and I allowed myself to be a victim. I thought quitting meant I wasn't good enough, that I was a failure. I let my boss plant seeds in my mind that I was weak. I let someone else control my thoughts about who I am. When I left with no job and no income, I was in control. I had taken my power back. I was no longer the victim; I was a victor. It took several months to figure this out and accept it. It took many more months to thank God for the blessing He gave me. My boss was a gift, and I am very thankful to have received him in my life. I heard a saying once: God gives you pebbles before throwing a stone. He had given me pebbles for many years and finally hit me with a giant boulder. I realized that I was so strong that I wouldn't give up easily. I was good enough that I turned a crummy situation around into a successful, high-performing team. I love my former boss now because he gave me the keys to my destiny, without which I would not have launched out on my own.

My Gift to You

I have excellent news—you can learn from my lesson by applying these three principles:

> 1) **You have a choice.** In everything you do, you get to choose what is right for you. Do not be afraid of how others might judge you. There are no wrong choices for you; there is no failure. Every decision you make is the absolute right choice. Whether you go with your instinct, or

you are methodical in your thought process, each decision you make will prove to benefit you. To get further ahead, make a decision. Stick to it if it feels right, and divert if it does not. Do not dwell on a choice you feel you made in error; instead look for what is possible because of the choice you made.

2) **Define yourself.** Others do not define who you are. Others will try to convince you that you are something you are not. Do not listen to them. Do not let negative people influence you. Take time to write out who you are, your personal credo, your values. Make sure your actions support those values. You are enough the way you are today. Surround yourself with like-minded people who support who you are. Find positive people to be with every day. Positive people and positive thinking attract other positive people and thwart off negative people. And do not define yourself by money. Focus on what you want, and you will have an abundance of life and wealth.

3) **Take care of your health.** A healthy body and mind are essential. Often people get caught up in negative situations; their minds replay messages like a broken record, they feel trapped, and they neglect their health. Your health may be a sign that it is time for

change. If you have been feeling ill and cannot determine the cause, look inside yourself, because the answer is there. How you focus on your health helps or hinders your quality of life. You want an excellent quality of life in order to be creative, productive, and happy.

Life is a roller coaster, and it is meant to be that way. Every difficult situation is intended to expand who you are as a person. My boss allowed me to get to know myself better than I would have on my own. He pushed me to seek new experiences that I never would have considered, and he stretched me beyond my comfort zone. He gave me gifts in disguise. These blessings inspire me to live my dream of helping women entrepreneurs be successful in growing their businesses and teaching the effects of a positive attitude on success, leadership, and employee engagement.

What gifts are in disguise in your world?

About the Author

Jennifer Darling is a passionate, dynamic speaker with a mission to break down negative barriers into positive ideas in business and leadership for women. She has over twenty years of experience in sales, marketing, management, and personal development for companies such as FOX, NBC, CBS, and Comcast. She holds a master's degree in management and a bachelor's degree in advertising and promotion. She is a member of the National Speakers Association, Toastmasters, and a Jeffrey Gitomer Certified Advisor. Jennifer is a published author, trainer, and sought-after speaker.

Jennifer has helped thousands of businesses and hundreds of salespeople have their best years ever through her speaking, coaching, training, and workshops. Often referred to as a "professional problem solver," she has the unique ability to uncover complex business problems and turn them into money-making opportunities. She gives audiences the tools and strategies they can use the same day to make immediate and long-lasting, positive changes.

Jennifer is a high-impact speaker with a proven track record for success both on and off the stage. She makes sales and leadership fun by tapping into the feminine moxy. She empowers and inspires for a results that are positively successful! Visit www.DarlingCoaching.com for a free gift!

TURNING THE PAGE AT FIFTY

My Journey to Balancing Mind, Body, Spirit, and Passion—Inside and Out

Dr. Elsie Crowninshield

> "Success? I don't know what the word means. I'm happy. But success, that goes back to what in somebody's eyes success means. For me, success is inner peace. That's a good day for me."
>
> **Denzel Washington**

In 1996, at age thirty-two, my husband and I relocated from the East Coast to Pasadena, California, both of us wanting to finish our master's degree in nursing. Shortly after graduation in 1999, we moved again, this time to the San Fernando Valley, where our first child, David, was born (now sixteen). Two years later our daughter, Morgan, was born.

We both began our new careers, and just when I thought we had it all together, in 2010 an event happened that would change my world forever—and drastically. My life literally turned upside down when I suddenly realized that my marriage was ending. A sense of fear overwhelmed me, knowing I would soon become a single mother of two young children.

The worst part of all was being without my children every other week, when they were with their father; it was essentially the loss of my family unit. This left me with lots of down time and hours of thinking about how I could turn this period of my life into something positive. After making some really poor decisions, I decided to focus the time and energy I had in the evenings and weekends without my children to learn about social media and technology.

As the World Turns, So Must Elsie

I was determined that if I was going to make it on my own in this big world, I had to change with the way of the world. I bought a 27-inch Apple iMac, iPad, and three iPhones, one for each of us. Once I learned how to operate a Mac and became proficient, I chose my path: I decided to get a doctorate degree in nursing practice (DNP). I was influenced by other nurse practitioners and nursing leaders, and I knew this would further my career and open new doors for my future in nursing practice and nursing leadership.

Dr. Elsie Crowninshield

I was specifically focused on any opportunities that would lead to improving my children's lifestyle. I wanted nothing less than the absolute best of everything for them, including a nice home with great schools in a safe area. My heart hurt terribly when I didn't have both of them with me for those long seven-day stretches every other week. The sense of emptiness was indescribable; it was the most painful period in my life, and I knew I had to somehow find a way to overcome it. My passion was to be an accomplished nursing leader in Los Angeles and share my wealth of knowledge and experiences, coaching and mentoring as many nurses as I could, watching them develop under my leadership while I continued to oversee projects, programs, and people.

I began reading a few good self-help books on dealing with divorce. The most powerful advice I read was to focus on goals that are achievable, concentrate on the positives in your life, and follow your heart and what you are passionate about. Although my kids continued to be my first priority, I learned quickly by doing just that, and it began to fill the void and loss I felt during those first painful few years. I convinced myself that 2011 would be the year I set my own personal dream into action and set sail to the next part of my life journey.

The desire to pursue my DNP actually had begun years ago when I was practicing as a cardiovascular acute care nurse practitioner, shortly after I graduated

California State University Los Angeles with my master's in science of nursing. As I began studying for my doctorate, I set my goal to graduate by the age of fifty. My children were nine and eleven at that time, and I was (and still am) the nursing director of critical care services and two cardiac telemetry step-down departments for a large trauma center in Southern California. My desire was so strong and my heart and soul were on fire, so I got ready, got set, and went for it. As I read through multiple university applications in California, I literally reset my brain, telling myself, "GO GET YOUR GOAL."

Pursuing the Goal

Three program options were available in California: San Diego, San Francisco, or San Bernardino. So, the journey began, with transcripts, the application process, recommendation letters, and a personal interview at Loma Linda University in San Bernardino County with the doctors running the program, and finally in spring 2011, my acceptance letter. Over the next three years, I would embrace this change and follow my passion, which was to obtain my Doctor of Nursing Practice.

Unaware of my personal journey and goals, or why my desire to do this was so strong, initially I had a tough time convincing my kids why I needed to spend so much time away from them pursuing something they saw as a "takeaway" from their "mommy time."

They did their best to try to understand, though, and amazingly they eventually became my best supporters, which meant the world to me. In summer 2011, my twelve-year-old son decided to reside with me full-time, while my daughter continued with the every-other-week schedule. This was another transition! It was a major adjustment for all of us, yet the kids were resilient and continued to cheer me on.

Professionally, the support I received was overwhelmingly positive. I was accepted by the senior leadership in my hospital, which was necessary for anyone enrolled in a doctorate program while working full-time. Our family vacations soon became four days a semester spent in seminar sessions, four times a year, staying in hotels close to Loma Linda University. Monday through Friday morning routines became waking up at 4:30 a.m., participating in online posting in chat rooms, and finishing papers. I squeezed in an occasional trip to the gym prior to two separate school drop-offs in different valleys in Los Angeles, followed by a full day's work. Evenings became visits to random Starbucks, where I worked on papers and online postings while waiting for my daughter's dance class to finish. Then it was home to cook dinner and spend time with my son. Late nights into the early morning hours were spent reading, writing manuscripts, completing and posting assignments due by midnight—my only undisturbed time.

Turning the Page at Fifty

In 2013 I began a journey toward living a healthier lifestyle. Part of this involved a decision to move from condo living to a larger home in suburbia. Realizing I could not take on such a big change while in the doctorate program, I submitted a one-year leave of absence request, which thankfully was honored. I learned a key life lesson from this event: It is okay to take the time you need for your well-being, and it's okay to take a break when life throws you a curve ball. Perfection is not always necessary, and relocating in the midst of my program was ultimately the best decision I ever made for my children and myself.

Turning the Page

In June 2015 I graduated from Loma Linda University with my doctorate in nursing practice. Shortly thereafter, I began engaging with people from within my community. I knew the time was right to begin searching for people who could help me begin the next stage of my journey: a focus on wellness and becoming an entrepreneur. Wanting to involve myself in ideas and products that would help me "turn the page at fifty," I took a class on essential oils. There I learned how using these products could help my children and me live more healthfully and vitally.

I decided to become a consultant for Doterra Essential Oils. I began using their Vitality Lifelong Pack daily supplement system and quickly started feeling better on the inside. Next I incorporated aromatherapy and oil diffusers in my home and at my office. In addition, I joined Rodan and Fields as a skin care consultant; these products changed my skin like no other product I had ever used before.

These products and companies are unbelievably successful, and the intriguing thing is that my business with these product lines is mostly on social media. As a wellness advocate and nurse practitioner, my goal is to help people take care of themselves and help them achieve their own wellness by sharing what a difference it can make for them in their lives. I am passionate about holistic healing and natural ways of caring for ourselves, so I continue to search for new ways to engage professionals to see the value of incorporating this into their everyday practices.

In November 2015, I joined a marathon training group at the Paseo Club in Valencia, California. Melanie Hyde Vovk coached me to reach my goal of running my first Surf City Half Marathon on February 7, 2016. I began meeting more and more businesspeople in the Santa Clarita Valley and eventually I joined a Master Mind Business Group led by Sue Brooke Cowling. Knowing that I have always wanted to be an entrepreneur and share my wealth of knowledge with other master's and doctorate nursing students, she helped me design my own website—and most of all, she has inspired me to achieve success as I begin my own consulting business in healthcare as a wellness advocate.

Find your passion and your "why," no matter what challenges you encounter along the way. Success is not achieved by working hard; it is achieved by working intensely and passionately on something you want to achieve for yourself. Embrace your challenges with a positive attitude—it's *your* mind you have to convince. I promise you, it will be the best decision you will ever make!

Dr. Elsie Crowninshield

About the Author

Elsie Crowninshield is an entrepreneur in the healthcare industry, a doctor of nursing practice, an acute care cardiovascular nurse practitioner, and board-certified nursing executive. She has extensive clinical and leadership experience in operations as well as financial and project management for major medical centers in the academic, nonprofit and for-profit arenas. Elsie is known for mentoring and coaching nurses and students throughout their career.

Elsie offers consultation services and wellness advocacy and is focused on her journey to balancing the mind, body, spirit, and passion from the inside out for all healthcare professionals. She may be reached on the following websites:

www.elsiecrowninshield.com

https://www.mydoterra.com/elsiecrowninshield/#/

https://ecrowninshield.myrandf.com

CUES FROM THE UNIVERSE—BELIEVE

Charr Crail

We are all faced with a series of great opportunities brilliantly disguised as insolvable problems.

John Gardner

I finally had my dream job, the one I'd been working toward during a career I loved as a professional photojournalist. I was a picture editor at one of the top ten metropolitan daily newspapers in the country. But over time I realized that I didn't belong there; it was not *my* dream job, and I didn't know what to do about it.

What happened next was divine. I recognized the signs because I'd been at that crossroads a few times before.

This time divine inspiration arrived in the form of a refrigerator magnet. While wandering around a local art store, I was seized by the message, "Leap and the net will appear." Yes! I could leap! But what was it that gave me that level of confidence? I remembered now: I'd been leaping all along.

Just days after I saw that magnet, I did take the leap out of my job with the newspaper and into the perfect dream—my own freelance photography business, which is still thriving well over a decade later.

I have often used the inspiration of a moment to determine my next move in both art and life decisions. I've relied on inspiration and leaps of faith all my life. While taking art classes in high school, I leaped into creativity. My art teacher never told me what to do as he did with the other students. He gave me the gift of freedom to trust my instincts and follow my own inspired journey while making art. He encouraged me to enter art competitions, where I won awards, and this buoyed my confidence.

I moved cross-country from Miami Beach to Laguna Beach at age nineteen with so little time to pack hardly anyone knew I left. In my thirties I had mononucleosis for a year and started over from scratch once I could get out of bed again. And I broke off a long-term relationship with a man I was completely in love with because I had to stand on my own and get out of his shadow.

We often have to make hard decisions. Sometimes they're a matter of survival; sometimes it's simply time to get happy.

Charr Crail

Looking back on my life, I realize that I experienced a series of magical, pivotal moments that served as divine inspiration on my journey to where I am now—in my happiest place.

On Valentine's Day 1979 I drove eight hours north from Southern California to Sacramento to begin a new life in a new place I knew nothing about. I was in my twenties, moving back in with my parents, and somehow I knew this move was right.

After a couple of weeks in Sacramento, I was ready for more. I decided the unemployment office was the perfect place to start looking for a job. The woman across the desk asked me what I did.

"Well, I took art classes in school and worked in a retail shop," I said, "but *I'm a photographer.*"

The words tumbled out so fast I didn't even know I was going to say them. They even shocked me. "I'm a photographer" had zero bearing on reality. In fact the closest I'd ever come to being a photographer was taking a high school photo class and having two hammy girlfriends with cameras who constantly wanted pictures of themselves.

The woman lowered her chin and smirked. "We don't get too many photography jobs here," she said.

The next day a miracle occurred: The woman at the unemployment office called me back. "You won't believe it. A photography job just came in! Go see Mr. McGee at Mr. McGee's Old Time Photos in Old Sacramento, today if you can."

Cues from the Universe—Believe

The real-life Mr. and Mrs. McGee had a wonderful old-time portrait photo studio in historic Old Sacramento, a popular tourist destination.

I probably didn't say more than eight words during that interview. I simply sat, listened, and smiled broadly as Mr. McGee explained the job. I think he liked my smile. He hired me, and I started the next day.

The gig was dressing people up in Old West costumes and posing them with stern expressions, as if the photos had been taken at the turn of the century. I still use the tips and tricks I learned during those amazing days about photographing people, which is still my favorite thing do.

It was a great job, and working with the McGees taught me so much, but eventually I outgrew it. I wondered how to evolve. Then, while helping my roommate with her college video class final at Cosumnes River College, something happened.

"You need to take Gene Stephens' journalism class at Sac City so you can get an internship at KCRA," I heard a stranger say to someone at the far end of a long hallway, referring to a local TV station.

Those two people never knew I was there, but hearing those words inspired me to quit my job, use all my savings to pay six months' rent in advance and convince my parents to give me a tiny monthly sum so I could go to Sacramento City College and study journalism. College, an experience I had steadfastly avoided, was suddenly beaming with glorious golden light in my now-inspired imagination.

My life had a brilliant new direction and purpose—TV journalist!

On the first day of class, in walked Dr. Jean Stephens. Standing in front of a room full of eager journalism students was a perfectly coiffed, white-haired woman dressed head to toe in lavender. Her dress, her purse, shoes, and the delicate lace handkerchief in her hand, were all the same shade—not a Gene at all. She introduced herself and then said something I've never forgotten.

"Look around you," she told us. "Look around at all the people in this room. If you continue in this field, these are the people you are going to know for the rest of your life. You'd better be nice to them, because one day one of them may have the opportunity to hire you—or fire you."

Decades later I can say she was absolutely correct.

Doc, as she was widely known, was selling the *Associated Press Stylebook*, our class textbook, from her desk at the school newspaper office. She asked me, "Do you write?"

I said, "Not really."

She asked, "Do you take pictures?"

"Yes, I do," I replied with a smile.

Within minutes Doc had signed me up to be a staff photographer on *The Express*.

One of my favorite visual memories of all time happened only moments later when I was heading toward the exit and saw a large picture window. Behind it nine guys—the photo staff—were all smiling at me, one of them gesturing with his index finger to come in. They'd heard that a girl had joined the staff and wanted to meet me right away. So began perhaps the most magical period of my life.

I was now part of something big and true—lasting friendships, community, the deep satisfaction of having a great and meaningful mission—and most of all I was having fun while learning. Those wonderful guys took me under their wings and taught me how to develop film, how to print in the darkroom, how to see and capture the world around me. We all wanted to bring out the best in each other, and the constant inspiration flowed freely as we discovered the richness of a journalistic point of view while telling stories with our cameras.

I discovered joy and purpose. My inner ambition was awakened to seek a life as a photojournalist, something I felt was already inside me since I was a child watching my father, the newspaperman, on the job.

My own professional entry into the world of newspapers happened when Doc recommended me to a local paper in desperate need of a six-week fill-in photographer. In fact, they were desperate enough to hire me without ever meeting me or seeing my work. They trusted Doc and that was enough. Six weeks turned into three thrilling years as I learned on the job how to be a bona fide professional. This gig on a modest paper became the center of my world and taught me volumes I could never have learned any other way. I was in love with photojournalism and continued for years at several papers before leaping from a sure thing into my own great wide open.

If I hadn't trusted and followed my inspiration during a series of unexpected opportunities, I may never have walked the perfect path and experienced the perfect life lessons I needed to be exactly where I am right now—inspired and ready for more.

I learned this a long time ago: Inspiration isn't just an aha moment. Inspired action often follows those moments. Now, as a seasoned professional, a visual storyteller, and a teacher in the same college that gave me my start, I love to inspire and encourage others to trust, embrace, and express their uniquely creative selves.

About the Author

Charr Crail has been a photographer and artist all her life, and a working professional photojournalist for over twenty-five years. She specializes in photographing people, entertainment, creating imaginative photo illustrations, and teaching.

Charr is an oft-published photographer in both newspapers and magazines and has won numerous awards for her photography and artwork worldwide.

Charr speaks to professional groups and colleges about photography and offers workshops at her photo studio in Sacramento in art and digital imaging for both beginners and pros.

Learn and see more about Charr on her website, www.charrcrail.com.

IN HIS HANDS

Michelle Calloway

"I've learned that people will forget what you said, people will forget what you did, but people will never forget how you made them feel."

Maya Angelou

I had no clue that I was on a path of self-destruction. I was a follower, and I didn't care much about anything. My parents made me go to church every weekend whether I wanted to or not. I didn't have faith in God, though; I was just going through the motions. I was fourteen years old.

Things would never be the same for me after he walked into the room with those gorgeous blue eyes and sparkling smile. Time stood still for me. I had never laid eyes on anyone so perfect before. I know no one's actually perfect, but I'm telling you, my heart skipped a beat and I felt all tingly inside.

His name was Chuck. It turns out he was my angel, sent to me from the God I didn't even know yet. Perhaps that's why I felt all tingly inside when I first experienced his presence. Let me tell you a bit of our story.

It took two years of being friends before we officially began dating. He was four years older than me, but remember, I was only fourteen when I was first awestruck by this guy. He taught me how to drive a stick shift, balance a checkbook, and make good decisions by thinking instead of reacting. Most importantly, he taught me how to love God.

We ended up getting married when I was nineteen years old and he was twenty-three. Life was really, really good. I married my best friend, got a fluffy white puppy, and began traveling the world. Four years later I gave birth to our first daughter, and eighteen months later I gave birth to our youngest daughter. It didn't get much better than that. It was a joyful, peaceful life. And then—it began to change.

He wouldn't wake up for days. I didn't know what to do. He tried to push himself, but he had nothing left to push with. He began missing so much work that I was afraid he was going to lose his job. I begged him to see a doctor. Finally he did. The tests came back normal. Now what? He finally found an endocrinologist willing to take on tough cases. Over the next six years, my husband was a human guinea pig. They finally diagnosed him with an autoimmune disease called Kleine-Levin Syndrome.

Ultimately he had to leave work and go on medical leave. His body was slowly taking him captive. His organs were all off balance, altering his chemistry, bone density, digestion, cognitive ability, and moods. It was awful watching him suffer. There wasn't much I could do except show him love and support, and keep the kids as quiet as possible so they didn't disturb him when he was sleeping.

He and I would pray together, begging God to intervene and heal him. I Corinthians 10:13 in the Bible states: "God is faithful; he will not let you be tested beyond what you can bear. But when you are tested, he will also provide a way out so that you can endure it." I held tight to that Scripture as we earnestly prayed together night after night after night.

One night, as Chuck was writhing in pain, I cried out to God to make it stop. Why would God allow such a good, loving man to suffer so much? Why wasn't He healing him? This had gone on long enough! I put on the proverbial boxing gloves and had it out with God!

I called Him a liar! Told Him I couldn't trust Him! Told Him that I never wanted to speak to Him again, that I didn't need Him! I walked away and turned my back on God. After all, He wasn't doing anything to help the situation anyway!

Time went on, and Chuck's health continued to deteriorate. I cried daily, but I never let him or the girls see me. I tried to be strong for my family, to be as positive as I could. It was exhausting. My heart was completely broken and full of darkness. Chuck's outcome was bleak as the doctors shrugged their shoulders, not knowing how to help him. It had been six long months since I stopped talking to God, and I had never felt so hopeless, or so alone.

It was humbling crawling back to God. I sobbed at His feet and begged Him to forgive me for my arrogance and my outrage against Him. I knew in my heart of hearts that it was *His* decision to intervene or not. It was *His* decision because He is the all-knowing, all powerful, Creator of this universe and all that live in it! Who was I to think that I could tell *Him* what to do and how to do it?

I was a wreck. The one person I loved the most was dying, and I couldn't do anything to change that. God could—however, I had to come to grips with the idea that God knows best. His ways are not our ways, as it says in Isaiah 55:8. Another verse, Ephesians 3:20, reminds us that God is capable of doing far more than we can ever imagine. That's because *He* is God, and *we are not*! It was a tough life lesson for me, but I would much rather have God with me and suffer loss, than *not* have God with me and still suffer loss and feel hopeless and alone.

My dependence on God and my faith grew after that pivotal moment in my life. Chuck ended up passing away. Before he died, though, he made peace with the fact that God is in charge. We both learned that it's best to surrender your will to Him and be content with "what is" than to be in a constant state of defiance and struggle proclaiming "what should be" based upon our human understanding and expectations.

It was an incredibly sad and devastating time for me. The love of my life was gone, but I lived on, so I knew there must be a purpose for my life. Scripture says, "We know that in all things God works for the good of those who love him, who have been called according to his purpose" (Romans 8:28).

So I dove in! God and my girls were all I had left. I knew better than to put my faith in man, because I just witnessed first-hand that people let you down. They don't mean to, but sometimes they get sick and die! I knew that I had to put *all* of my faith in God. He is the only one that doesn't leave us (Deuteronomy 31:8), or fail us. In fact, He wants "good" for us (Romans 8:31). He loved us enough to send His only Son to die for our sins (I John 4:9). Who does that? No one else I've ever met.

From that point on, I told God that I was *all in*! I promised Him I would be faithful and obedient to whatever He wanted. His purpose was my purpose, even though I had no clue what that was. I made a proclamation to God that I would serve Him in whatever capacity He called me to.

Fast-forward ten years. God sent me a new husband, who loves God and treats me like a queen. I've raised my girls, and they are making lives of their own. Having lost my job during a recession, I went back to college to gain insightful knowledge about digital media. Soon thereafter I was introduced to mobile augmented reality technology, which overlays virtual content on top of real life objects; the virtual content is viewable through mobile smart devices.

God began to prompt me to make some radical changes. In obedience, I followed those promptings, and with my husband's support, we started downsizing. Surprisingly it felt really, really good to get rid of most of our "stuff." It didn't stop there though. God prompted us to go further and sell our home. So we did.

Then He went even deeper and prompted me to start a new business focused on augmented reality technology. That's where it got tough! I had run a small business before, but I had no experience being an entrepreneur with a scalable business model. I was unsure how to proceed, and it sounded like a lot of sacrifice and hard work. We would need investors, and we would probably need to relocate. What if I failed?

Remembering the promise I made to God after Chuck died, and knowing that God's will is perfect (Romans 12:2), my husband and I dove in and began the journey of a lifetime. Two years later, here I am, writing this chapter. Having uprooted our lives and sold most of our possessions, we are living out our faith for a purpose much higher than ourselves. My faith in God's perfect plan is what inspires me to press on. God is with us! The future is His!

About the Author

Michelle Calloway is a graphic designer turned visionary. After being introduced to mobile augmented reality (AR) in 2014, she became devoted to studying and developing AR technology while incorporating her love for graphic design. She moved to the San Francisco Bay area to launch her new start-up, REVEALiO, which uses augmented reality to make (printed) cards "come alive" with video and call-to-action buttons when scanned with a mobile device.

Michelle believes she was "called" to build this business to get AR into the hands of everyone all over the globe. There's no better way to introduce augmented reality to the masses than through printed cards that "come alive" with a personal video message. It's amazing, fun, and deeply impactful!

Ultimately Michelle believes that her AR tech business will fund ministry and support missionary workers all over the globe as they bring the message of hope and salvation through our Lord Jesus Christ to those who don't know Him.

SOARING TO NEW HEIGHTS

Nancy Darst

"Only those who will risk going too far can possibly find out how far one can go."

T.S Eliot

Nancy put every ounce of energy with her body quivering in that 5'4" frame to complete, not the tenth but the eleventh pull up that would take her to a higher level of conditioning. Nancy pursued her sport with full passion—never giving up, practicing with sore muscles, ripped, callous hands, and determined to become a champion gymnast.

The champion knows what the three Ps of Preparation, Practice, and Perfection lead to: winning! Nancy was stellar at working toward Olympic gold. Achieving gold meant setting priorities, making lists of goals to pursue, and then measuring the improvement. Nancy asked questions, researched the best in the world of gymnastics, modeled the Olympians, and expected to receive the same rewards as the champions she looked up to.

Getting better day by day and working harder and harder until the payoff—Nancy knew she had to win first place in district, state, and then regional competition to qualify for the national AAU Junior Olympics.

Routines required ten consecutive tricks in trampoline (which included doubles and double twisting somersaults) with perfect precision. Fifteen years old and ready, Nancy beat the competition, winning first place at district, followed by first place in state, and first place in regionals thus, earning her a spot in the nationals. *A dream come true . . .*

The chance to soar to new heights at the National AAU Junior Olympics sparked a new sense of excitement and achievement inside Nancy. Going to nationals and making the finals was confirmation that she could do what she put her mind to and fostered in her a deep appreciation for the other competitors.

After returning home, Nancy began training even harder for the next major competition, now with a clear vision on how to win. The United States Tumbling and Trampoline Association (USTA) competition arrived, and Nancy won first place in all the events: tumbling, trampoline (compulsory and optional), plus the synchronized event with a partner. Now she was soaring even higher and met all her goals.

The winning athletes were so excited to find out that World Class Gymnasts and Trampoline Champions were available to share their expert advice, show new tricks, and give coaching tips. From the sidelines, Nancy's parents, grandmother, and brother all watched nervously as a coach demonstrated a difficult trick for Nancy to try. The trick she dreamed of accomplishing was the double front flip with a half-twist. Nancy had seen it performed and had visualized it in her mind, but had never tried it because her home gym did not have a mechanic with a twisting safety belt.

The coach gave Nancy a warm-up routine with several tricks to prepare for the big trick. The safety belt was put on and Nancy listened to the coach and heard the words, "Get comfortable with the height and stretch your arms up, then go into the front somersault and stay tucked one-and-a-half times around; next open up to see the 'X' on the trampoline bed and finish the last part with the half-twist."

Nancy did as he instructed and executed the double front flip with a half-twist perfectly. She was amazed and performed it a few more times. The coach was so impressed that he said she could do it and the safety belt was removed. Normally this trick took weeks or months to master so it would be ingrained in the athlete's muscle memory and was very difficult.

Nancy wasn't quite sure that she was ready to have the belt removed, but she knew if she didn't learn it then it would be a long time before she would get another opportunity. In the heat of the moment and without hesitation, Nancy did what the coach instructed.

The belt was off, and Nancy sprang into action. She performed the double front flip with a half-twist to perfection. When Nancy completed this difficult trick, she was excited, amazed, and ready to do it again. Nancy repeated the maneuver two more times—and then it happened.

Nancy over-rotated, got lost in the trick, and saw the ceiling instead of the "X" on the trampoline bed so she ducked her head and landed on the back of her neck. The coach ran over to her, yelling, "Nancy, lie down and don't move!" She replied, "I know I can do it—I want to try it again!"

As Nancy did as the coach instructed, she realized she couldn't feel her hand or her right arm, and she knew at that moment the accident was serious. Everyone looked on in quiet disbelief as Nancy waited for the ambulance. After X-rays at the hospital, the doctors put her in a neck brace and told her to see her doctor in St. Louis after the feeling in her hand returned.

Nancy's parents blamed themselves and regretted taking Nancy to the competition that was an eight-hour drive away. The next day Nancy's doctor told her mom to take her to the hospital to see a specialist. After extensive X-rays they told her not to move and put her in a wheelchair, and she was immediately checked into the hospital. Feeling scared for the first time, Nancy cried as she heard that a vertebrae had cracked, another one was twisted and was a fraction of an inch away from cutting her spinal cord. Nancy needed surgery; however, the doctors didn't want to operate on her since she was so young. Instead Nancy was put in traction for two weeks and left the hospital with a body cast from her waist to the top of her head, framing her face like a TV set. The cast would remain on Nancy for three months.

During her recovery, Nancy met with a tutor to keep her studies up. The one thing on her mind was hearing the doctors say, "You'll never be able to do sports again" and telling her she was lucky she didn't die or become paralyzed.

However, Nancy knew what was inside her, and giving up was not an option. She decided to soar to a new height—one that would prove everybody wrong. With determination Nancy planned her comeback. Nancy knew recovery would be a long journey and appreciated being surrounded by an amazing family. When Nancy felt down, her brothers lifted her spirits with their jokes and ridiculous pranks, and would get her laughing. Ultimately, Nancy's relationship with God provided her with an undeniable faith that she would heal.

Three months later the cast came off, and Nancy was fitted with a neck brace. She wore the neck brace for

Soaring to New Heights

six weeks and returned to school with instructions not to do any sports. After the six weeks, the next set of X-rays were taken, and the doctors said it was amazing that her neck healed up so well. They suggested swimming to strengthen, condition, and add flexibility to her muscles. Swimming at the YMCA pool every day worked so well that when Nancy's doctors conducted their final evaluation, they gave her the go ahead to play sports again. Everyone knew it was a true miracle, and Nancy understood that her strong faith coupled with the treatment of the doctors enabled the gift of healing that took place. Nancy was overjoyed and knew she wanted to be involved in sports again, but she decided her trampoline days were over.

With her injury behind her, Nancy used the three Ps: (preparation, practice, and perfection) and continued to train hard in gymnastics. She applied for and received a gymnastics scholarship to the University of Colorado, where she competed, studied, and traveled with her team all over the country, and became a nationally ranked gymnast.

Although Nancy never made the Olympics, she held close to her heart the realization of how close she came to never doing sports again. The experience taught her with God all things are possible. "Getting better day by day, and working harder and harder until the payoff" took on a whole new meaning for Nancy. The faith to move on, not give up, and be committed to always soaring to new heights became her motto for life. SOARING TO NEW HEIGHTS stands for SOARING:

S—Start
O—Out
A—Affirming
R—Resilient
I—Intentions
N—Nurturing
G—Guidance

Nancy has never stopped soaring. She went on to become a professional aerialist and showgirl for the Biggest Circus on Earth and went on to master the flying trapeze. She performed throughout the US and internationally. Highlights included performing at Tivoli Gardens in Copenhagen, Denmark; the Circus World Championships in England; and the Monte Carlo Circus Festival. After the competition Nancy had the opportunity to dine with Prince Albert and Carey Grant. She was really soaring high and it felt like a dream—all her perseverance certainly paid off! Nancy continued to challenge herself and went on to perform in ice shows, then created and performed in her own magic shows.

In life we experience many different paths, and sometimes we even crash and burn. If you learn how to apply the SOARING formula, you too can live your passion and experience the heights your human spirit can go.

About the Author

Nancy Darst is a performer, speaker, educator, and author. Through her experiences in sports, gymnastics, flying trapeze, and the amazing art of magic, Nancy has developed an informative and magical performance and program that motivates and inspires others.

Through her life, Nancy has had amazing achievements but also faced many adversities where she learned to overcome them with her perseverance, determination, patience, and faith. She never gave up, and she learned to cope when the odds were not in her favor.

Along with First Class Magical Entertainment, Nancy developed a program known as Creative Magical Solutions so she could help others through their setbacks and transitions. Nancy guides others through areas such as goal-setting, letting go, moving on, overcoming fears, and making things happen in one's life.

Let Nancy assist you to discover your hidden talents and start developing your potential so you can add more fulfillment, confidence and satisfaction and to your life in a fun and creative way. To find out more about Creative Magical Solutions, visit www.NancyDarst.com.

MEET THE AUTHORS

Visit http://www.DiscoverYourIBooks.com to read more about all of our wonderful authors and connect with them!

BECOME A FEATURED AUTHOR IN THE DISCOVER YOUR "I" BOOK SERIES

Real Stories from Real People to Inspire and Ignite Your Soul

This book is the first in a series of Discover Your "I" compilation anthologies. Discover Your "I" Books is a collective book project featuring real, inspirational stories from real people.

As an author, you will share your personal story of your journey from where you were to where you are now. Reveal your passion and your expertise and your struggles to your successes! If you have a story to tell that will inspire someone in some way, please consider publishing in one of our future books. You can find out more, and apply, at http://www.DiscoverYourIBooks.com.

Please watch for other books in the Discover Your "I" Book Series, or find them, at http://www.DiscoverYourIBooks.com.

A few titles include the following:

Soaring to New Heights

Discover Your

- *Intimacy*
- *Intuition*
- *Impact*
- *Image*
- *Immortality*
- *Individuality*
- *Investments*
- *Intention*

MEET SUE

Sue is the founder of Discover Your "I" and co-creator of the *Discover Your "I"* book series. She is a small business mentor, speaker, educator, author, coach, and idea innovator. After surviving a car accident and finding herself with a depleted bank account at the age of forty-four, Sue describes "being hit by a truck" as the moment that changed her life forever. She reclaimed her identity and built successful businesses, all on her own.

Sue enjoys working with small-business owners and people who have dreams to start a business. She has the unique gift of coming up with innovative ideas and finding opportunities where no one else would think to look.

As a passionate advocate for anyone who may have lost their identity, she strives to empower and inspire them to live their passion and never to give up on their dreams, no matter how crazy they may seem!

Sue believes that everyone has a story that should be told. Giving people an avenue for sharing their own stories and encouraging others to share theirs is dream that has come to fruition in her Discover Your "I" book series.

> *If you're living your passion, and doing what you love to do, then you've discovered who you really are!*
>
> **Sue Brooke,** *Discover Your "I"*

www.ingramcontent.com/pod-product-compliance
Lightning Source LLC
Chambersburg PA
CBHW071628080526
44588CB00010B/1316